KNOWING THE
HOLY SPIRIT

(THE SPIRIT OF GOD)

Pastor Nnaemeka C. Uchegbu

iUniverse®

KNOWING THE HOLY SPIRIT
(THE SPIRIT OF GOD)

iUniverse books may be ordered through booksellers or by contacting:

iUniverse
1663 Liberty Drive
Bloomington, IN 47403
www.iuniverse.com
1-800-Authors (1-800-288-4677)

Because of the dynamic nature of the Internet, any web addresses or links contained in this book may have changed since publication and may no longer be valid. The views expressed in this work are solely those of the author and do not necessarily reflect the views of the publisher, and the publisher hereby disclaims any responsibility for them.

Any people depicted in stock imagery provided by Getty Images are models, and such images are being used for illustrative purposes only.
Certain stock imagery © Getty Images.

Scripture quotations from the Holy Bible, King James Version (Authorized Version). First published in 1611. Quoted from the KJV Classic Reference Bible.

ISBN: 978-1-5320-8258-0 (sc)
ISBN: 978-1-5320-8259-7 (e)

Library of Congress Control Number: 2019913674

Print information available on the last page.

iUniverse rev. date: 10/31/2019

Contents

Foreword

From ancient times, most societies have practiced some form of "spirituality". Many communities pursued their own brand of worship based on cultural set of beliefs without reference to any other outside source of power or insight. In doing so, they created for themselves what the Apostle Paul described as "a form of godliness, denying the power thereof" (2 Timothy 3: 5-7).

But a generation that claims to believe in God needs a correction to this kind of self-styled "spirituality" that clearly distracts people from what true spirituality entails. So, in "Knowing the Holy Spirit", Pastor Nnaemeka Uchegbu provides a very comprehensive consideration of the work of the Holy Spirit of God. This is the source of power necessary for people to experience a genuine spiritual life.

Pastor Uchegbu does not offer mere platitudes and slogans in this book; he does a very detailed, scripturally-based treatment of the Holy Spirit in all aspects of His work. The work of the Spirit in both Old and New Testaments, the impact of the spirit coming in power at Pentecost, the gifts of the Spirit and the ongoing working of the Spirit in believers...and more...are addressed in detail.

Without the Holy Spirit we are dead in the water. Without

the Holy Spirit all of our religious activity is just going through motions and rituals. Pastor Uchegbu has reminded us of the fundamental necessity for the Spirit to flow through us in order for us to lead a true life in Christ. No one else can substitute this. The Holy Spirit must be present, or we will go nowhere.

"Knowing the Holy Spirit" is an inspiring overview of how God works in our lives. God will bless you as you open your heart to a greater and deeper move of the Spirit in you. May God use this book to help you enter into a fresh, dynamic season of your walk with Him.

Bishop Timothy A. Johnson
Executive Director,
Minnesota Church Ministries Association

Epigraphs

"For what man knoweth the things of a man, save the spirit of man which is in him? even so the things of God knoweth no man, but the Spirit of God." (1 Corinthians 2: 11)

"Wherefore I give you to understand, that no man speaking by the Spirit of God calleth Jesus accursed: and that no man can say that Jesus is Lord, but by the Holy Ghost" (1 Corinthians 12: 3).

"The entire Bible is about the good news of the coming kingdom of God. It consists of an interesting collection of divine mysteries wrapped around God the Father, God the Son, and God the Holy Spirit through whom Jesus Christ the Messiah was revealed to the world" (Nnaemeka Uchegbu).

Introduction

At the center of the Christian faith are certain doctrinal claims that have over the centuries attracted fair questions from believers in God and non-believers alike. And because some of these sacred claims form the basis of Christian beliefs, they deserve clarifications for the sake of disabusing the minds of skeptics and secular critic.

A few foggy areas that attract critical but honest attention here include such issues as, "The existence of God", "Who is the Holy Spirit?", "Is Jesus the Son of God?", "The resurrection of the Lord Jesus", "The concept of the Holy Trinity", and "Are Heaven and Hell real?" These are just few questions amongst others.

These issues are indeed numerous and cannot appropriately be dealt with in one format alone. As a result, the theme of this book will zero in only on the concept of the divine Holy Spirit. In doing so, my treatment of the subject matter will focus primarily on what the holy Bible teaches concerning him.

Many literary works on the divinity of God are already in print. But, most of these books, either by design or in error concentrate mainly on the persons of God the Father and God the Son. But in this book, a third, often not-much-talked about, supernatural Being, whose role in the family of the divine Trinity is not merely equivalent but equal to that of the Father and the Son, is the person of interest. His name is the Holy Spirit.

In introducing the Holy Spirit, I have endeavored not to adopt the usual, confusing, religious talking-points which have often complicated matters of faith rather than simplify them. I have also, consciously resisted the idea of dumping exaggerated, Christian talking-points or opinions on a subject as truth-demanding as the Holy Spirit, who by every standard deserves the most honest representation.

Instead, through some un-biased research, supported by numerous scriptural references, I have compiled in very simple terms from the perspective of God's word, several evidences of the reality of the existence of this note-worthy spiritual Being who most Bible scholars harmoniously refer to as the Holy Spirit.

Those who desire to know the Holy Spirit, will find enough relevant scriptures in this book to help them understand the nature and characters which equate him with God the Father and God the Son. They will also come to appreciate the things that qualify this notable figure as an indispensable friend of the Christian and the church.

This book, "Knowing the Holy Spirit" does not claim to be an "All you need to know" presentation on the subject. But I hope it presents a clearer perception of this other dimension of the divine Deity who possesses the same attributes with God the Father and God the Son. So, I pray that reading it will assist in dispelling any former wrong views held about the nature of God, as what it reveals will shine more light on the mysteries behind God's real and true identities.

Even though the Holy Spirit has been the least known person of the Divine family, the person who needs a closer walk with God will find that knowing him will open the eyes of any person who desires a fulfilled spiritual journey in life. This is because, through his operations, the supernatural power, presence and gifts of God are revealed to Christians for the benefit of the body of Christ.

Therefore, the quest to know the person of the Holy Spirit should begin with the knowledge of the word of God, which is the Bible. This will enable a deeper understanding of the secret things hidden since past ages, which God reserved, but reveals to those faithfully seek his face.

God is the source of all knowledge, and apart from him, no human effort can effectively explain the nature of the "Holy Spirit". No imagination of the carnal mind or depth of human knowledge can adequately explain his nature. Only God can reveal him to whom he wills. That is why he is God (Deuteronomy 29:29).

Bearing this in mind, the urge to know the Holy Spirit should be even more appealing to the humble seeker who will soon discover that his teacher in this great adventure is the All-knowing God, whose Spirit is the willing revealer of all truth.

This book is written in very simple literary manner and language with the hope that it will appeal to believers who want to unlock new levels of divine understanding and thereby enter into God's supernatural blessings. It is also for the comparative theological analyst or honest critics who is exploring concrete facts in order to prove or disprove the existence of the Holy Spirit.

I trust that studying it with deep meditation and support from the various biblical scriptures, will bring revelation-knowledge and spiritual refreshment. And I pray that the divine Holy Spirit, the inspirer of the true and useful knowledge, will give a deep understanding of himself to all who seek him.

ONE

In the beginning

The word, "huge" does not come close to describing the size of the earth. And when the innumerable stars in the firmament, the number of the sand on the sea shore, the volume of water in the ocean, the multitude of trees in the forest and the population of humans are included, the desire of knowing who created all these things becomes very appealing to the inquisitive mind.

But how did all these come about? Who or what put them together? The question of the origin of the universe is a matter that has existed from the time man began to reason. And while there is a consensus by all parties concerned that the universe was "formed" by pre-existing "forces", there is a sharp disagreement as to the exact method of its formation, depending on which side of the discussion a person belongs.

Yet, whether the earth was created by "God", as is believed in Judeo-Christian circles or by "Brahman", the metaphysical reality and creator-deity of the Hindus, somebody or something was responsible for it. A class of scientists claim it was formed by an explosion which they refer to as the 'Big-bang, yet another group of biological theorists maintain it was by natural process due to evolution. Thus, from the dawn of human knowledge, the war to claim credit for who, what or how this complex world-system came to be has raged contentiously between divergent schools of thought.

While all these different theories on the origin of the earth have their points, the evidences behind the "creation-theory", supported by numerous un-erring biblical scriptures, make the most convincing argument. The Bible story strongly states without any ambiguity that the earth, including the outer space, all living and non-living things, originated from the specific acts of divine creation.

What this means is that the entire universe was spoken into place by the Supreme Deity during a six-day period of creation, as is stated in the Bible. In fact, the opening lines of the book of Genesis, which is the first book of the Bible, presents this argument in the most emphatic way, stating that,

> *"In the beginning God created the heaven and the earth. And the earth was without form, and void; and darkness was upon the face of the deep. And God the Spirit of God moved upon the face of the waters. And God said, Let there be light: and there was light" (Genesis 1: 1-3).*

This statement confirms what those in the school of Creationism believe, which is that God created the entire universe. Thereafter, he followed with orderly putting things in place, whether in the heavens or on the earth. And lastly, he made man in his image and likeness and placed him a beautiful Garden of Eden, to take care of the things he made. Unfortunately, this claim by Christians and others who believe in one supreme God, has over time continued to elicit challenges from skeptics and secular critics.

And, while the idea of creation remains the central theme in the religions that believe in the supreme deity, heretics, the apostate, the heathen and secular critics have a completely different notion. Evolution-scientists, for instance, maintain that whatever exists came about due to transformation of simpler species that occurred, giving rise to higher forms.

Their view is that the universe began when certain variations occurred in non-organic substances. As a result of these variations, they say that organic life-forms were produced by a natural process. Then, as time progressed, these simpler life-forms further changed into more complex forms through random alterations, as they were influenced by their environment.

Another group of scientists hold yet a different notion. They claim that this universe came about due to a random act of cosmic interaction of pre-existing, subatomic substances. They state that it was the product of this reaction that gave rise to a habitable earth. This is known as the "Big Bang" theory.

Consider these statements on the "Big bang" theory taken from Space.com, a premier blog of the exploration and astronomical news. The excerpts refer to the origin and age of the universe, and it says,

"The Big Bang Theory is the leading explanation about how the universe began. At its simplest, it says the universe as we know it started with a small singularity, then inflated over the next 13.8 billion years to the cosmos that we know today".

"While we can understand how the universe we see came to be, it's possible that the Big Bang was not the first inflationary period the universe experienced. Some scientists believe we live in a cosmos that goes through regular cycles of inflation and deflation, and that we

just happen to be living in one of these phases".
(The bold letters and italics are mine).

These findings really do not throw any new light on how the universe came into being. What such inconclusive scientific claims continue to do is mock the firm, un-altered idea of creation by a Supreme Deity. They have not proved to be reliable alternatives by any measure, even though they constitute consistent views from notable scientific critics, most of who are atheists.

Instead, they continuously introduce more controversies to an issue, which they sought out to resolve. The only meaningful facts they have brought to light is the idea of pre-existing matter from which simpler forms evolved to more complex ones. In making this argument, astronomists point to the presence of energy which aided the "Big Bang" that signaled the dawn of time. But how the initial matter or primary energy that initiated the original reaction came from is not explained. So, their theories have continued to leave humanity with more questions than answers.

As for the biologists who cling to the theory of "evolution and natural selection", nothing new has happened since the early 19th century when the French naturalist, Jean-Baptiste Lamarck, first proposed the idea of biological evolution. And from the times of Charles Darwin (1859) and Alfred Russel Wallace, who published their findings on the organic evolutionary theory to this age, no baboon has evolved into man.

So, while it is true that a person's environment, the food he eats, special chemicals and radiation they come in contact with can lead to variations in that life, such changes can either be harmful, beneficial or neutral. In the case of creation by evolution, this argument falls flat because it assumes that it was only beneficial that one time, since no more apes have evolved into man thereafter.

Despite these human flaws, some scientists still maintain their theory of evolution or persist in the claim that cosmic collision caused in the origin of earth. All in all, these groups continue to reject the idea of divine creation and denigrate the act of divine intervention. It is among them that you find people who say there is no God. By extension, they also disparage the idea of Jesus as God's Son and say there is no person as the Holy Spirit.

Such condemnations are not new. They have existed since medieval times and are even retained in modern scientific curriculum. However, if anything has evolved over time, we can point to some scientific theories that changed from what classical scientists once held to be sacrosanct to new knowledge which modern scientists now acknowledge existed but where not known to them in the past.

For instance, classical theorists believed the Atom to be the smallest particle of matter. This was held to be true for many centuries until Sir Isaac Newton discovered smaller units known as electrons, protons and neutrons. All this time, the word of God did not change but remained the same from eternity to date.

The truth is that science, which is a natural concept, is too much in conflict with itself to be solely relied on to explain spiritual matters. Even among notable cosmologists, there is no agreement whether the universes existed before the erstwhile "Big-Bang, or the situation is reversed. And even in this modern age, Earth-theorists maintain that the earth is flat. But for long, the great Greek philosopher, Aristotle, supported by other Greek scholars, taught that the earth was round. While Sir Isaac Newton, by his own theory, suggested that the earth was oblate-spheroid.

Christopher Columbus was a brutal Italian explorer and tyrannical colonizer credited with discovering peoples and nations during his numerous expeditions. He was even acclaimed for finding viable sailing routes and continents that were not of prior knowledge to others before him including the Americas.

Columbus' stories, could have formed another body of hypothesis on the origins of man and those lands if he wished. But the truth is that the people and lands which European history books said he discovered were already in their place, established by God (and not evolution or the Big Bang), before he reached them.

This is because, there is not much difference between how these unbelieving scientists view God and the way Columbus dealt with the Jamaican Islanders he encountered after his ship was stranded there in February 1504. Half of his crew had abandoned him, and the locals denied him food.

But he knew about an impending lunar eclipse. So, desperate and starving, he lied to the Islanders that his god was coming with his wrath to deal with them on his behalf for denying him food. And on the night 15th of February 1504, the eclipse occurred, causing the frightened Islanders to rush food and other provisions to him. This is how the skeptic scientific world deals with ignorant humanity.

Christopher Columbus' approach was one deceptive model that viewed God as a god. A god who defends tyrants and callous people. He was an acclaimed sailor knowledgeable with the science of the oceans and the wind. Yet he lied that an eclipse was the action of his god at work and historians sold the idea.

Thus, when you consider Columbus model of god, the new information now associated to his false claims on groundbreaking discoveries of peoples and lands, and match them against some philosophical models on the same issue of God, creation and nature, which have also evolved, even if slowly, it becomes comfortable to trust the eternal, reliable, inerrant ways and word of God which have remained constant.

This is Because, "from the beginning" when God said he

created the universe, to this very time, his word has remained the same. The word of God notes that there are things which mankind does not know. And it states that there are things which he can know. But this is not so compared to scientific theories most of which are "suggestions" and "estimates" that change with revelation of deeper knowledge

> *"Likewise the Spirit also helpeth our infirmities: for we know not what we should pray for as we ought: but the Spirit itself maketh intercession for us with groanings which cannot be uttered. And he that searcheth the hearts knoweth what is the mind of the Spirit, because he maketh intercession for the saints according to the will of God. And we know that all things work together for good to them that love God, to them who are the called according to his purpose"* *(Romans 8: 26-28).*

According to recent evidence by cosmologists, human understanding of the universe is still evolving, even if they say it is doing so significantly. But the word of God does not evolve. It has remained the same since the dawn of time, doing what it says it will do, strictly to the letter.

That is why Science cannot explain how a person can get healed only by looking at a bronze serpent. Neither can it account for the feeding of five thousand people with only five loaves of bread and two fish, with twelve baskets of left-over food after everyone present had eaten. This is an issue of faith. And only God can make this clearer.

The children of Abraham were slaves in Egypt for four-hundred years. When their bondage became harsh, they cried to God and he came to their rescue. God's plan was to take them out of Egypt and bring them into the land of Canaan as he promised Abraham.

But the journey to Canaan from Egypt became wearisome for these Hebrews in the wilderness. And they began to speak discontentedly of God and murmured against Moses. They soon forgot God's goodness and he delivered them from Egypt. They distrusted the One that fought for them against their enemies, gave them quail and manna, and provided them with water in the desert.

As a result of their rebellion, God sent a plague of serpents to afflict them. Because they rejected the word of God and murmured against the bread of eternal life which nourishes those who feed on it by faith, God sent fiery serpents among them. And many of them perished from the poison from the serpent-bite. Then, God provided them miraculous relief in the form of the brazen serpent which he instructed Moses his servant to make.

> *"And Moses made a serpent of brass, and put it upon a pole, and it came to pass, that if a serpent had bitten any man, when he beheld the serpent of brass, he lived" (Numbers 21: 9).*

The serpents that bit the children of Israel in the wilderness were real life serpents. And all the victims could have died from the poison or the pain of the bites. But those who were doomed to die but looked up in faith to the bronze serpent which Moses made as God instructed him, all survived the attack. However, those who did not look up, but rather focused on their wounds, died from the deadly bites of sin.

The bronze serpent that was lifted up in the wilderness was a symbol of Christ's offer of salvation to all who will believe in him. Human salvation comes by looking up to Jesus and trusting that he will save. That is why it is written in the Gospel of John that,

"And as Moses lifted up the serpent in the wilderness, even so must the Son of man be lifted up: That whosoever believeth in him should not perish, but have eternal life" (John 3: 14-15).

By following the word of God, a righteous person with no education can understand what many intelligent philosophers without God cannot unscramble. That is why human knowledge is still at the level of relying on computer-models to track hurricanes and monitor their route, speed and power.

But with the All-knowing God, things are different. He knows the source of the wind and its direction. And he does not need the services of any meteorologist to second-guess the direction of a hurricane, a Tsunami or tell the devastation any of them could cause. He can tell it all even before they happen.

That is why the academic mind alone finds it difficult to understand how it is possible to receive healing just by focusing on the brazen serpent. These skeptics will never comprehend how the sting of a serpent can be rendered painless or the poison of an adder can easily be neutralized by just looking on a brazen serpent. But it happened. Because with God, all things are possible. He even suspends natural principles to give spiritual laws pre-eminence.

What secular critics do not realize is that the healing of those bitten by the serpents was not obtained because the victims looked to the brazen serpent. But in looking up however, they were expressing unshaken faith in God who dwells in the heavens. By lifting up their eyes in faith, these Hebrew children connected in obedience to Jehovah Raupha, the God who indeed is the healer.

Even so now, the sinner who looks up to Christ the Savior receives salvation through faith. All these are mysteries which can only be made plain by God who is the creator of man and the universe. It may sound crazy to the skeptics and those who teach that evolution, rather than creation brought life into existence. But the reality of the matter, that God is the creator, remains unchanged.

God's infallible word truly supersedes whatever facts evolution-theorists can ever assemble. But sadly, some ardent cosmologists continue to argue against the truth of the Bible even in areas where evidence from science now completely agrees with faith. What these and other fervent advocates of evolution hypothesis on creation do not realize is that God created science and there are now consistent scientific evidences that support the theory of Divine creation.

Almost everything God spoke to Jeremiah at the beginning of his prophetic ministry, happened while he was alive. On the death of King Solomon, the Nation of Israel split into two feuding kingdoms. The northern part was called Israel and the southern kingdom became known as Judah. This was a very tough time for both kingdoms. They had started to decline politically, decay morally, and spiritually descend into apostasy due to the many idols that made their way into their nation as a result of the many heathen wives King Solomon married.

> *"Before I formed thee in the belly, I knew thee: and before you camest forth out of the womb I sanctified thee, and I ordained thee a prophet unto the nations" (Jeremiah 1: 5).*

Jeremiah lived and prophesied for forty years during the reigns of the last five kings of Judah. God spoke severally times to him and through him, calling his people to repentance otherwise become slaves. They did not repent, and for it, they suffered captivity under the Assyrians as well as the Babylonians. Israel suffered exactly as Jeremiah had told them by the word of God.

"Lo, I will bring a nation upon you from far, O house of Israel, saith the Lord: it is a mighty nation, it is an ancient nation, a nation whose language thou knowest not, neither understandest what they say. Their quiver is as an open sepulchre, they are all mighty men. And they shall eat up thine harvest, and thy bread, which thy sons and thy daughters should eat: they shall eat up thy flocks and thine herds: they shall eat up thy vines and thy fig trees: they shall impoverish thy fenced cities, wherein thou trustedst, with the sword. Nevertheless in those days, saith the Lord, I will not make a full end with you. And it shall come to pass, when ye shall say, Wherefore doeth the Lord our God all these things unto us? then shalt thou answer them, Like as ye have forsaken me, and served strange gods in your land, so shall ye serve strangers in a land that is not your's" (Jeremiah 5: 15-19).

God does not operate by guess work. Everything he said would happen from the time of creation or from when men began to call upon the name of the Lord and through the mouth of his prophets, have either completely come to pass or about to happen as he said. That is why the theory of creation makes more sense than the theories of evolution and natural selection or the erstwhile Big-Bang theory.

From the beginning of what man regards as dawn of time, the word of the Father of all creation has remained firm. Times and seasons may have come and gone, human society, traditions and cultures may have changed from what they used to be, but God's ageless word, his covenants and promises have remained the same.

Consider the Israel of this generation and you will have cause to trust the God who claims he created them for his name-sake. Some of what he spoke concerning Israel more than two thousand, five hundred years ago, through Prophet Isaiah is happening right in this generation. God has always left Israel a remnant and used them to replicate the nation, not once or twice. Just when the world thinks it is over with Israel, God arises to their rescue and restoration, according to his unfailing love and word of promise, which he spoke in the beginning.

> *"Hearken unto me, O house of Jacob, and all the remnant of the house of Israel, which are borne by me from the belly, which are carried from the womb: And even to your old age I am he; and even to hoar hairs will I carry you: I have made, and I will bear; even I will carry, and will deliver you" (Isaiah 46: 3-4).*

> *"And ye shall seek me, and find me, when ye shall search for me with all your heart. And I will be found of you, saith the Lord: and I will turn away your captivity, and I will gather you from all the nations, and from all the places whither I have driven you, saith the Lord; and I will bring you again into the place whence I caused you to be carried away captive" (Jeremiah 29: 13-14).*

Even in this modern age, no one can dispute the prophecies about Israel. That the modern State of Israel is small in geographic size, few in population and surrounded by very rich Arab enemies is not in contention. Yet, they are amongst the six strongest nations in the world, with the strongest economy in the Middle-East. They boast of the strongest military might in that geo-political zone and are ranked among the world's great nations in science, agriculture, technology and other fields of knowledge. So, while the claim by creationists remain the same, the theories by evolutionists continue to change from generation to generation.

It has become sarcastic to the point of humor that modern evolutionists no longer express much confidence in their "god of the laboratory". In years past, they stoutly defended their ape to man model. This lasted until honest, modern scientific findings began to reveal that there were indeed no genetic bases for supporting the much-touted link between humans and chimpanzees. Now, no one knows what the next scientific talking point will be on this issue.

Yet the word of God spoken about the process of creation, has remained the same. As clearly stated in the book of Genesis, God said he created man in his image and likeness. But with animals, he said he formed them according to their own species. From this statement by God, honest scientific findings now confirm that humans and apes are not related.

So, while evolutionists (who have no need of God) and who also are fervent advocates of atheism continue in their endeavor to refute available evidences of biblical truth, unbiased scientific methods state categorically that no one kind of organism can change to another by genetic mutation.

Thus, no one should worry that different groups of evolution "theorists" continue to oscillate from one view-point to the other in their concerted effort to explain the origin of the universe and disprove God. The cheering news is that God's word has remained authoritatively the same since the time he commanded the universe into place and caused his prophets to record it as so in his word.

And, thank God for many godly-minded scientists, through whose research, those who once held contrary biblical opinions, evolved in their knowledge of the truth. One of such persons is the Oxford trained scholar, CS Lewis, whose adult conversion from atheism to Christianity is well chronicled in his apologetic classic, "Surprised by Joy" (Harper Collins). Other skeptics can learn from him.

If anyone is looking for evidences of God and the Holy Spirit, the birth of Isaac to Abraham and Sarah who were past the age of child-bearing, the exodus event of the children of Israel from Egypt, the unprecedented parting of the Red Sea and the miraculous dividing of River Jordan to enable the children of Israel cross over to the land of Canaan, all carry the finger prints of a supreme, transcendental intervention.

When these evidences are added to the testimony of the praise-induced, collapse of the walls of Jericho, just to make way for God's covenant children to pass through to Canaan and the almost impossible victory secured by Joshua as the sun stood still for him to accomplish a divine assignment, no one will be in doubt of the supernatural finger of God.

Gideon's victory with a three-hundred-man army over the multitudes of the Midianites, is a miracle only God could have worked. Again, the deliverance of Israel from the destruction plotted against her by Haman the son of Hammedatha the Agagite, in the courts of King Ahasuerus should teach skeptics that there is God.

PRAYER POINTS.

1). O God that begins all things, start a new thing in my life today, in Jesus name.

2). Alpha and Omega, teach me to start well and to finish well, in Jesus name.

3). O God my Father, you are my creator, do not forsake me, in Jesus name.

4). O God that speaks and it comes to pass, speak into my situation, in Jesus name.

5). O Lord reposition the things in my life that have been displaced, in Jesus name.

6). Holy Spirit, let your calm overrule any confusion in my life, in Jesus name.

7). Holy Spirit! let your presence overthrow any disorder in my life, in Jesus name.

8). Holy Spirit, brood-over my life and let all dark shadows flee, in Jesus name.

9). Voice of God, speak now and change my condition, in Jesus name.

10). Light of the living God, brighten the countenance of my face, in Jesus name.

11). Faithful God! restore the Eden I have lost through sin, in Jesus name.

12). O God, let my present and my future be better than my past, in Jesus name.

13). I crush the head of any serpent on assignment to deceive me, in Jesus name.

14). I reject every fruit that will take God's glory away from me, in Jesus name.

TWO

Does God Exist?

The first-step to knowing the Holy Spirit must begin with acknowledging the existence and true nature of the Sovereign God. So, who really is God? In Judeo-Christian theology, he is believed to be the Creator and sustainer of the universe. He is the supreme Being that is All-Mighty in power, perfect in knowledge, understanding and wisdom, and great in goodness.

He is a spirit Being with infinite mind who in his majesty, splendor and greatness, possesses all things, lacks nothing and is graciously benevolent. He is the One God who exists as One substance though in three persons as God the Father, God the Son and God the Holy spirit. This concept is the core essential upon which the Christian faith is built.

> *"For there are three that bear record in heaven, the Father, the Word, and the Holy Ghost: and these three are one. And there are three that bear witness in earth, the Spirit, and the water, and the blood: and these three agree in one"* *(1John 5: 7-8).*

So, to deny any aspect of his divine nature, is to declare that God is a fraudster and a liar. This will not only demean the sacred integrity of God's divine nature as believed by Christians but present their confidence as trust that is wasted on matters of no relevance.

Achieving this, no doubt, has been the prime objective behind the futile efforts by skeptic-scientists and agnostic philosophers who ridicule the Christian faith. All their motives focus on discrediting the idea of a Sovereign Deity and thereby demystify the nature, character and identity of God, whose finger-prints are irrefutably reflected in every facet of creation.

From many centuries past, the claim that there is no God, but a concept of "God-delusion", has resonated in prominent, non-God believing, academic circles. This was the stand of Richard Dawkins. And other astute atheists like Daniel Dennet, Sam Harris, and Christopher Hitchens share or shared the same opinion.

Some people in this academic club have even written books with such sarcastic titles as *"The Portable Atheist"* (Christopher Hitchens), *"The Faith of a Heretic"* (Walter Kaufmann), *"Atheism: The Case Against God"* (George Smith), *"God in the age of Science: A Critique of Religious Reason"* by Herman Philipse.

No doubt, these sophisticated books make interesting literature, especially with all the fine academic assumptions that make them intellectually appealing to those who hold the same view. But beyond that, the ideas they advocate are inadequate in providing credible proofs against the numerous, obvious and convincing, evidences of the existence of God.

Atheists say there is no God. Their argument is that if there is God who claims to be all-loving, all-powerful and of good moral nature, why would he permit natural disasters or even allow innocent children to die in wars, of hunger, cancer and other incurable sicknesses?

They ask why will a compassionate God who claims to be patient and full of goodness let souls roast in horrible torment in eternal hell-fire because they did not believe in him? And they also ask that if God is the Sovereign creator of all things, as he claims, why would he not show himself to humanity?

Well, one of the most fundamental errors atheists make is to believe that if God cannot be found in their "small", human mind-set, then he does not exist. It is funny how someone with faith that the sun will shine, and in the beauty of the spring-flora, will denigrate the One who made these things, because they cannot capture his face in their minds or with their "precision" telescopes.

I do not know how many people in the past ever physically met the Queen of England. But all the people in the colonies governed by the British empire who were provided with the atmosphere of peace, protection and economic growth believed she was their ruler. So, we see how easy it is to bow to human authority while refusing to accept the supremacy of the creator of all things.

> *"If we receive the witness of men, the witness of God is greater: for this is the witness of God which he hath testified of his Son. He that believeth on the Son of God hath the witness in himself: he that believeth not God hath made him a liar; because he believeth not the record that God gave of his Son" (1 John 5: 9-10).*

Yet, no one within this group has been able to come up with any reasonable "laboratory proof" of his non-existence, just as they cannot say which came first, the galaxy or the stars. This is why it is absurd to continue to listen to theories and probabilities from those who argue that the Supreme God does not exist.

By extension, the same class of non- believing-scholars have reasoned that the idea of the Holy Spirit is mere human creation designed to advance religious purpose. So, they maintain there is nothing like the Holy Spirit. That is why to understand anything about the Holy Spirit, a person must begin with acknowledging that God exists. This begins with a good knowledge of the Bible. This is where anyone can find true knowledge of who God is, his true nature and what he does, among other things.

Who is the Christian God?

God is the eternal, righteous being who exercises kindness and justice to all who seek him. He is the Self-Existent One who has always been. He was not created by anyone or thing, but exists by himself, with his Son and the Holy Spirit. The three share the same glory.

> *"Thou art worthy, O Lord, to receive glory and honour and power: for thou hast created all things, and for thy pleasure they are and were created. (Revelation 4: 11).*

He is the supreme Being who exists in an eternal, self-sustaining manner and is independent of his creation for his nature. He is the prime initiator of all things who did not have to be initiated. He is the one who created man for his glory and delights in all that are called by his name.

By his immeasurable grace, he extends unmerited favor and unconditional love to all righteous believers. And by his unfathomable mercy, he forgives sinners who come to him through his Son Jesus Christ, granting privilege of eternal life to those who will remain till the end.

While many agnostics, unbelieving scientists and Atheist-philosophers have an academic disdain for the person who religious people describe as God, honest, humble people who have genuinely experienced him are too glad to associate with him. This is because, finding God brings love, peace, protection, and faithfulness which give hope beyond measure in time of need.

Only a credible Being with such incomparable, supernatural power as God, can accomplish what he says he would do and has done. He calls the things that do not exist, and they come into being as if they originally existed. He speaks to the wind and it obeys his voice and the stormy waters listen to his command.

The supreme God is the only one who could have given impossible victory to a young shepherd boy called David, over the experienced, Philistine war-giant known as Goliath. This giant stood before Israel in the battle-field. And for forty days and nights he ridiculed their King and blasphemed the One they called God. And this went on un-checked for all those scary-days, until God showed his power through David, the son of Jesse, the Bethlehemite. This is the Christian God.

The Bible relates that the plans to the exquisite temple built by King Solomon in Jerusalem, Solomon's un-matched wealth and wisdom, the sacred works of prophets Isaiah, Jeremiah, Hosea, Amos, Daniel, and other great-men and women of the Bible, were incredible acts possible only by divine, supernatural interventions. To think that all what the prophets spoke have either come to pass or are about to happen, makes the word of God a reliable dossier of spiritual magnitude.

And when these are added to the sacred way by which Jesus was conceived, his wisdom, anointing and the grace that was upon him, his healing miracles, the feeding seven thousand people with a young lad's lunch-pack of five loaves and three fish, the manner of his crucifixion, death and resurrection, no one is left with doubt why the finite mind cannot comprehend the nature of the infinite God except by his revelation.

Before the wind-vane came into use, people could not always rightly determine the direction of the wind. But with better understanding and knowledge man came to appreciate the importance of the wind-vane. So, anyone looking for scientific evidence to prove the existence of God or his Holy Spirit will not find any until they return to God and his word. Because, while no laboratory experiment can locate his origin, no human theory can explain his image or camera capture a selfie with him.

Does this mean that science, philosophy and the quest for knowledge are not important? Of course not. In fact, every one of them has played vital roles in shaping society in one epoch or the other. However, any Christian who believes in God must realize that in matters of religious faith, reason must never be in contention. So, whenever faith and reason are in conflict in the life of a believer, faith must prevail.

Even by natural human methodology pilots do not learn to fly by working as farm-hands. No, they go to an aeronautic institute. In the same vein, anyone who desires knowledge of the intelligent creator of this complex universe and its contents cannot find any better source than the Bible. God's word is still the richest source of information about him and his nature.

So, till those who contest the reality of the person, character and nature of God, acknowledge that the human brain is limited in its understanding of spiritual matters, it will not be un-common to find people who say that God does not exist. And with that group in place, there will always be a segment of society who continue to challenge the existence, origin and nature of God.

But thank God for the wealth of undeniable evidences in

the Bible which clearly explain and support the involvement of a higher Being in the work of creation. The information about how he called the sun, moon and stars into existence and placed each in the firmament for its specific purpose is irrefutable.

From the time God created the heavens and the earth as the Bible said till now, everything has been as he designed it. The birds still fly in the air, the fishes and the great sea creatures still live in the waters, while the beasts of the forests still make their homes in the wild, as in "the beginning" when God created them.

And while available evidence shows that science has been useful in many areas of life, there are several grey areas where it has not proved to be very smart. In the issue of grasping and controlling certain, ordinary natural phenomena such as drought, hurricanes or typhoons, there does not seem to be any imminent scientific solution.

Consider the conflicts existing within the scientific community about some common natural problems. For instance, while one group of scholars believe in the theory of climate-change, another group swears by the data and findings from their laboratories that nothing like that exists. In this day and age, what science dishes out depends on which side of the political isle that sponsored the research.

Such apparent mishandling of important issues makes it even more difficult to concede to the repugnant positions of evolutionary theorists. Moreover, their alternatives are too unconvincing to withstand the compelling creation model stated in the Bible. If their hypotheses cannot as much as adequately solve natural problems on the earth plain, how can their views on issues of faith be trusted.

Yet, the argument continues to go back and forth about how the universe came to be and who created the earth. And while evolutionists hang to their crumbling argument on the human ancestry of apes theory (suggesting that man evolved from apes), those who support the creation model, which states that God created man in his image and likeness, point to the intelligent design associated with creation as evidence of intervention by a higher-Being with perfect knowledge. And that is who God says he is.

From this perspective, we understand from the better, most reliable and consistent creationist-model that humans were indeed created by God in his image and likeness. As a result, they are clearly distinct from the animal family, to which the apes and other beasts of the forest, who were also formed by God, belong.

So far, all the proposals by evolution scientists concerning the creation of the universe and man have remained mere bogus claims peddled predominantly by atheists who generally say there is no God. Creationists can boldly say this theory has no basis because, since the touting of the idea of the man to ape evolution, all the evidences backing up these claims have been mere probabilities.

If then, Science is this much in disagreement with itself on concrete natural issues, how can it be fully trusted as a reliable standard for dealing with spiritual concepts and supernatural matters. Spiritual truths indeed, can only be spiritually discerned.

God gives the knowledge of them to those who humble themselves before him. The world indeed is complex, and knowledge is tough to obtain. But the Christian God makes all knowledge available through the Holy Spirit, to those who, without any bias, honestly desire to know him.

He is Omni-potent, Omni-present, and Omni-scent in nature. Along with the Son and the Holy Spirit, he created the universe and all that exists in it. And he has authority over all his creation. So, the only other persons in heaven and on earth that share this divinely-inherent heritage as God the Father, are the Son and the Holy Spirit.

"And Jesus came and spake unto them, saying, All power is given unto me in heaven and in earth. Go ye therefore, and teach all nations, baptizing them in the name of the Father, and of the Son, and of the Holy Ghost: Teaching them to observe all things whatsoever I have commanded you: and, lo, I am with you always, even unto the end of the world. Amen" *(Matthew 28: 18- 20).*

No one says that the wind does not exist because it cannot be seen. People generally agree that the sun, the moon, and the stars exist because they see and feel their presence. Yet in the mind of some skeptic-scientists, the Sovereign God of the Bible, who formed the sun, moon and stars, and who knows their exact position, names, age and number, is considered non-existent because their methodologies cannot find any proofs.

Well, when God told Adam that sin will result in death, he sinned and died. And from the day that he sinned, shame, fear, hardship, sickness and other forms of wickedness lead to death, entered the world. Since then, man died spiritually, and death of the physical body also became a common occurrence.

From the time God said that unrighteousness living will lead to human destruction. And all those who lived contrary to God's commandment testify that greed, lust, lewdness, lying, abuse of God's goodness, flagrant perversion of divine blessings and contempt for order, attracted unbearable pain to their lives.

When the generation of Noah delved into wickedness, God sent a flood that wiped-out that old world. The only survivors were the righteous Noah and his family. Also, as the sin of Sodom and Gomorrah became exceedingly vile before God, he rained liquid fire on peoples of those cities. Evolutionists may not agree with these events. But their evidence remains till this day as proof that God exists.

The bible has a record of all things God created. And all the events of history that God choreographed are clearly recorded and can be verified. When the psalmist praises God because of the complexity of human nature, it is because he recognizes and appreciates the perfect intelligence of "the God of creation". That is why the disingenuous denial of Biblical truth will never cease to amaze anyone who has good knowledge of God.

It is no longer a big issue that skeptics are on the increase in their opposition against the idea of a supreme Being. For sworn un-believers against the concept of divine deity, it is understandable when they reject the notion of a sovereign God. But the problem arises when other religions that believe in One-God or other Christian denominations begin to express views that are inconsistent with what the Bible says about God the Father, the Son and the Holy Spirit.

The Unitarian sect, for instance, do not share in the concept of the Holy Spirit as they claim the idea is deduced from literal interpretation of the scriptures. The Jehovah's witness too say that The Holy Spirit is not a person comparable to Jehovah God and Jesus Christ. Instead, they describe him as God's active force.

However, in spite of these denominational variations, the opinion of the general church community, in line with her traditional Judeo-Christian beliefs, is an un-equivocal support for a six-day act of divine creation. And consistent with the word of God, as stated in the book of Genesis, the Holy Spirit was personally active during the entire process. Thus, the idea of who God is, in relation to the Holy Spirit can only be understood by going back to the Bible.

"In the beginning God created the heaven and the earth. And the earth was without form, and void; and darkness was upon the face of the deep. And the Spirit of God moved upon the face of the waters" (Genesis 1: 1-2).

In the opening verses of the Book of Genesis, Prophet Moses gave a vivid account of creation, beginning from the first moments when God began to put this universe in place. This account describes how God created the heaven and the earth by the power of his spoken word.

And when scripture is compared with the finger-prints of a higher, more intelligent designer and creator, the creationists claim of divine intervention is found to be more credible and thus more reliable than the postulations of un-believing-scientists or the hypotheses of atheist-philosophers.

For until now, there has still not been any homogenous consensus between these class of philosophers and scientists on the issue of creation. This is because the modules they apply to determine the reality of God and his nature have remained the same old, fallible, outside-the-Bible parameters. These indeed, cannot reveal who God is.

Knowledge is powerful. But when it is not properly exploited, it loses its power. Mere natural knowledge of any truth will most likely perverse that truth than preserve it. The same is true with knowing who God is and how he is related to the Son and the Holy Spirit.

Knowing the Holy Spirit and letting him take control of your entire spirit, soul and body, certainly causes him to step in and change former natural human attitudes and replacing them with spiritual zeal and power to accomplish uncommon feats. Such wonderful experience enables that Christian to live above their own problems while ministering to the needs of others.

Those who acknowledge that God exists, relate how peaceful their lives have become due to the salvation they received by believing in Christ through the work of the Holy Spirit. Through this fellowship with the Father, the Son and the Holy Spirit, a whole new dimension of Christian world view opens to those individuals.

But that has to start with recognizing that God exists, followed by the desire to fellowship with him. People have the tendency to do things by their own effort. But when they step out of the way and let God take control in their matter through the Holy Spirit, better results than anyone would have humanly accomplished are attained.

The truth is that God exists and the Holy Spirit too. Jesus spoke of God as his Father and the Holy Spirit. He spoke about them as real persons of essential divine essence and not just as spiritual forces. He referred to them as persons who talk, command, chastise, and have will. They love, groan, grieve and know what is in the human heart.

Names of God.

Apart from many incontrovertible biblical evidences, human life experiences are enough proof that God indeed, exists. Everything that exists has a name, names or titles by which it is described. And even somethings that exist but cannot be perceived, have names too.

So, God has names and titles by which he is known. As a living spirit-being who is capable of expressing personal and relational emotions, he has numerous names which are reflections, not just of his identity, but of his nature and characters.

Some of these names represent the titles by which he revealed himself to his chosen ones. And others are descriptions of encounters by men or women who experienced his saving grace, were over-awed by his presence or enjoyed his goodness at one time or the other.

Such names or descriptions point to God's personal qualities. They describe his acts and the way he relates to his creation, other issues important to him and they convey specific and personal meanings. All in all, God's names are rare, powerful and unique. They are also worthy of praise.

> *"Let them praise the name of the Lord: for his name alone is excellent; his glory is above the earth and heaven" (Psalms 148: 13)*

In ancient times, names conveyed deep information about a person. They described the circumstances of birth, identified with a person's place of birth and captured the family expectations on the day of naming. They also sometimes served as reminders to someone's purpose in life.

The ancient God of Abraham, Isaac and Jacob had a plethora of titles by which he was known. A few are described in this book and they include:

1). Elohim. (The Everlasting God; The All-Powerful God).

You can find this name in Genesis 1: 1). This is the name used to describe the God of creation. It is the title by which he is known as All-Powerful creator of the universe.

Prophet Isaiah invoked this title while re-assuring the children of Israel that their God whose word is eternal, neither faints, is never wearied, nor is he diminished in strength (Isaiah 40: 28).

2). El Roi. (The God who sees).

God sees everyone in all their circumstances. His fatherly compassion ensures that nothing about any of his children escapes him.

Hagar was an Egyptian handmaid of Sarai who became Abraham's second wife by the errors of human decision. But when Sarai dealt hard with her due to her arrogance, she fled from the presence of her mistress. But the angel of the Lord who found her by a fountain of water in the wilderness, encouraged her to return and submit to her mistress in humility. She was then with child for Abram.

After this encounter, Hagar called the name of the Lord who spoke to her in that place, "El Roi".

> *"And she called the name of the LORD that spake unto her, Thou God seest me: for she said, Have I also here looked after him that seeth me?" (Genesis 16: 13).*

> *"Yea, the darkness hideth not from thee; but the night shineth as the day: the darkness and the light are both alike to thee" (Psalms 139: 12).*

God indeed sees all things and in all places. Nothing or no one can hide from him.

3). El Shaddai. (The All-Sufficient One; Lord God Almighty).

The Almighty God is the undoubtable protector, defender and shield of those that obey him. He also is there abundant supplier of good things to those who trust him and diligently seek his face. Nothing is too much for God to do for his child.

> *"For a day in thy courts is better than a thousand. I had rather be a doorkeeper in the house of my God, than to dwell in the tents of wickedness. For the Lord God is a sun and shield: the Lord will give grace and glory: no good thing will he withhold from them that walk uprightly. O Lord of hosts, blessed is the man that trusteth in thee" (Psalms 84: 10-12).*

4). **Jehovah Raupha. (The God who heals).**

The name Jehovah Raupha was the title by which he revealed himself to Moses and the children of Israel when the multitude murmured about the bitter water they encountered in the wilderness.

> *"And said, If thou wilt diligently hearken to the voice of the Lord thy God, and wilt do that which is right in his sight, and wilt give ear to his commandments, and keep all his statutes, I will put none of these diseases upon thee, which I have brought upon the Egyptians: for I am the Lord that healeth the" (Exodus 15: 26).*

God is a healer. He promised that if his people obey him, he will save them from the diseases with which he plagued the Egyptians. In fact, most of the moral laws he gave them through Moses were designed to keep them from all manner of sicknesses.

Hezekiah was a person of faith and prayer who turned out to be faithful before God. Over a very long period in Israel's history, all the other Kings had failed God in his expectation of their obedience to his law and statutes. So, when Hezekiah became sick, God sent his servant Isaiah to him with the promise to heal him and did heal him.

> *"Turn again, and tell Hezekiah the captain of my people, Thus saith the Lord, the God of David thy father, I have heard thy prayer, I have seen thy tears: behold, I will heal thee: on the third day thou shalt go up unto the house of the Lord" (2 Kings 20: 5).*

5). Jehovah Jireh. (God shall provide).

God is the perfect provider for the needs of his people. No story in the Bible illustrates his loving kindness to mankind better than the event on Mount Moriah where he tested Abraham's faith by asking him to sacrifice the only son of his old-age.

While God was willing and intervened by providing a ram as a substitute for Isaac, on that sacrificial altar, he did not spare his only Son Jesus Christ from the pain, agony, anguish and death on the cross for the sins of all mankind.

> *"And Abraham stretched forth his hand, and took the knife to slay his son. And the angel of the Lord called unto him out of heaven, and said, Abraham, Abraham: and he said, Here am I. And he said, Lay not thine hand upon the lad, neither do thou any thing unto him: for now I know that thou fearest God, seeing thou hast not withheld thy son, thine only son from me. And Abraham lifted up his eyes, and looked, and behold behind him a ram caught in a thicket by his horns: and Abraham went and*

took the ram, and offered him up for a burnt
offering in the stead of his son. And Abraham
called the name of that place Jehovah Jireh: as
it is said to this day, In the mount of the Lord
it shall be seen" Genesis 22: 10-14).

6). Jehovah shalom (God is peace).

Those who obey divine instructions, are assured to enjoy the overwhelming peace of God. Gideon recognized that only God can give true peace to anyone who is on this earth. To commemorate this new-found peace, he built an altar to God whose peace is beyond human understanding.

> *"Then Gideon built an altar there unto the Lord,*
> *and called it Jehovah shalom: unto this day it is*
> *yet in Ophrah of the Abiezrites" (Judges 6: 24).*

> *"These things I have spoken unto you, that in*
> *me ye might have peace. In the world ye shall*
> *have tribulation: but be of good cheer; I have*
> *overcome the world" (John 16: 33).*

God always defeats his children's enemies in order to bring them peace. With God in the scene, believers are sure to enjoy inner peace and harmony.

7). Jehovah Tsidkenu (The righteous God).

This title denotes the righteousness of God. No man indeed is righteous. All human righteousness is as filthy rags. Only through the righteousness of Christ who is the perfect King and "the righteous branch", can a believer have access to God.

As the Messiah, Christ had all the nature and characteristics of God. So like God, he was holy and righteous, unlike the kings of the world and the people he came to save.

> *"In his days Judah shall be saved, and Israel shall dwell safely: and this is his name whereby he shall be called, The Lord our righteousness" (Jeremiah 23: 6).*

8). Jehovah Nissi (The Lord is My Banner).

The Lord is the believer's banner. Life on earth is war. And even today as was in the ancient times there are battles raging daily in the believer's life. In ancient times, nations raised their flags in the battle-fields while their armies fought from behind the commanders who carried the flags.

The banners were symbols of strength and deliverance. God is the God of deliverance who gives victory against the desires of the flesh. He is the Man of war and the Captain of the hosts who fights our battles against the enemy.

> *"And Moses built an altar, and called the name of it Jehovah Nissi: For he said, Because the Lord hath sworn that the Lord will have war with Amalek from generation to generation" (Exodus 17: 15-16).*

9). Adonai (Lord and Master).

This title denotes the Omni-potent character of God. His name is so powerful believers are warned against using it frivolously. This name is sometimes used in place of YHWH, which by Jewish tradition is considered too holy to pronounce.

> *"Thou shalt not take the name of the Lord thy God in vain; for the Lord will not hold him guiltless that taketh his name in vain" (Exodus 20: 7).*

10). **Jehovah Mekaddishkem (The Lord who sanctifies).**

> *"Speak thou also unto the children of Israel, saying, Verily my sabbaths ye shall keep: for it is a sign between me and you throughout your generations; that ye may know that I am the Lord that doth sanctify" (Exodus 31: 13).*

A person who is sanctified to the Lord is dedicated for holy service. He is a chosen person of royal priesthood that is holy unto God.

The names of God are evidences that he is a living, breathing Being. And even though he is a spirit-being, those who encountered him in very troubling circumstances have come to acknowledge that he truly exists. So, these names represent the titles by which he revealed himself those individuals or the names they gave him based on their experiences.

PRAYER POINTS.

1). O God that sees, have mercy on me and help me, in Jesus name.

2). Compassionate God, hear my cry and come to my rescue, in Jesus name.

3). My Master, help me to follow you without distractions, in Jesus name.

4). My Great provider, supply my needs according to your riches in glory, in Jesus name.

5). Peace of the living God, incubate my life, in Jesus name.

6). My Good shepherd, restore my thirsty soul by the still waters, in Jesus name.

7). My Good shepherd, take me to the green pastures, in Jesus name.

8). All powerful God, fight my battles all the time, in Jesus name

9). I am that I am, when you need me, send me, in Jesus name.

10). I receive the righteousness of Christ through the cross, in Jesus name.

11). Emmanuel, let me feel your presence all the time, in Jesus name.

12). All Sufficient God, I thank you for your abundant grace, in Jesus name.

13). Strong and Mighty God, defend your interest in my life, in Jesus name.

14). God Most High, I bow and tremble before you now and forever, in Jesus name.

THREE

Who Is The Holy Spirit?

All the books of the Bible speak graciously of the numerous activities of a third person of the divine God-head. In whatever book, or chapter he was mentioned, either silently or overtly, he was associate with divine power. So, there are several scriptures that provide glaring evidences of this distinct, supernatural Being who possesses same attributes as God, but is neither God the Father or God the Son.

While some scriptures describe this divine person as the Holy Ghost, others call him the Spirit of God or the Comforter. But the title by which he is mostly identified is the Holy Spirit. And when a closer look is taken on these titles, the respective names reveal his nature or specific function.

> *"For what man knows the things of a man except the spirit of the man which is in him? Even so no one knows the things of God except the Spirit of God. Now we have received, not the spirit of the world, but the Spirit who is from God, that we might know the things that have been freely given to us by God" (1 Corinthians 2: 11-12).*

"And God, which knoweth the hearts, bare them witness, giving them the Holy Ghost, even as he did unto us" (Acts 15:8).

The Holy Spirit is God's gift to the church. He is the Spirit through whom God calls sinners to Christ, converted and sealed unto the day of redemption. He is not Christ but another person from the same source who came to work on earth, on behalf of Jesus.

He is described as the Spirit of Christ, in the sense that he is the other Comforter and Spirit of truth, who also came from God to take the place of Christ and dwell eternally in the hearts of believers. In this role, he strengthens Christians in difficult times, encouraging, inspiring, persuading and testifying to them of Christ.

"But when the Helper comes, whom I shall send to you from the Father, the Spirit of truth who proceeds from the Father, He will testify of Me. And you also will bear witness, because you have been with Me from the beginning" (John 15: 26-27).

The Holy Spirit is a living member of the Sovereign family of God which includes the Father, and the Son. He is the promise of the Father to the church, which was fulfilled, following the finished work of Jesus Christ. He is the promise that Christ made to his disciples as a replacement of himself.

"And I will pray the Father, and he shall give you another Comforter, that he may abide with you for ever; Even the Spirit of truth; whom the world cannot receive, because it seeth him not, neither knoweth him: but ye know him; for he

*dwelleth with you, and shall be in you. I will
not leave you comfortless: I will come to you"
(John 14: 18)*

In the words of John Piper, in a video-message titled "The
Holy Spirit: He is God", the Holy Spirit is described as "The Spirit
of God in whom dwells all the fulness of divine deity".

He is the life-giving Spirit of God in man who represents
the person of God in every living being. He is in all living souls,
even within those individuals who say there is no God. He is the
essence of God that brings order in the church community, helps
in understanding God's word and gives strength to the Christian.

He is the spirit of truth that proceeded from the Father
to witness about Christ. He guides believers into God's truth,
convicts the world of sin, points men to judgment, leads them
to righteousness, and comforts the people of faith in this New
Testament dispensation of grace.

The Holy Spirit is same as God, not by creation but by nature,
for he proceeded also from the same eternal source with the Father
and the Son. And as the Son of God is same with the Father, even
so is the Holy Spirit equal with the Father and Son in character.

The Holy Spirit is a person.

The Holy Spirit is a real person, though not as in human
nature with fleshly body. But he is an entity with such personal
and relational characteristics as knowledge and emotions. So, he
is not a thing, but a living, spirit Being who can react to actions
which only living persons experience.

Although he is the least known of the three members of the
divine god-head, he nonetheless exists as an equal partner of the
triune entity. He is one of the three persons of the Trinity and

has existed from eternity with the Father and the Son before the universe was formed.

While skeptics dis-agree that there is even a Holy Spirit, some agnostics are fair-minded to describe him as a mere presence or consider him as a mystical force. But none of these really depicts the exact nature of this all-powerful dimension of the Sovereign God.

The Holy Spirit indeed, is a living person. He is not just an apparition created by the figment of human imagination, neither is a fleeting impression perceived in the mind of the religious man. He is a person, equal in all divine essence as God the Father and God the Son.

Christians are God's Temples, and the Holy Spirit resides in them. He is Christ's representative on earth and manifests in numerous tangible forms upon Christians, as he did on the first Pentecost when, as a mighty rushing wind, he rested upon the disciples, in Jerusalem.

He is the voice of God and the supernatural power that transformed ordinary fishermen into bold preachers, evangelists, and apostles. By his active, positive influence, men and women fearlessly proclaimed the gospel with a power that worked miracles and wonders wherever the early disciples ministered.

Man was created to do God's will on earth as it is done in heaven. Through a life of obedience and righteousness, Adam was designed to dominate the earth and replenish it. But when he failed to honor God's word and succumbed to the serpent's deceptive directives, he lost all that authority.

In this fallen state, he lost fellowship with God. The glory of divine protection departed from him and his wife Eve, and privileges attached to obedience also ceased. This was the awful condition of man on earth until God sent his Son on a redemptive mission which process culminated in the liberation of souls of fallen men and the reconciliation of man with God.

The Holy Spirit and Jesus were God's partners in that divine rescue program that has continued to rescue all those who come to believe in this glorious work of salvation. He is the one who reproves sinners of their sins, and after they are convicted and repent, these sinners receive forgiveness as the sins are washed by the blood of Jesus.

He feels the human heart-beat more than any living person does and sees beyond what any human eyes can perceive. He is a teacher who loves to bring to remembrance all things that Jesus taught his disciples in his word, is a great guide to all truth and desires to show believers the things of the future.

That was why Jesus personally introduced him to his disciples as the Spirit of truth who will abide with them forever. Christ also testified concerning the Holy Spirit, as the comforter who would proceed from the Father. He described him as co-eternal in nature and an equal partner with him and the Father in supernatural likeness.

He was prominent in Christ's birth, played predominant roles in his life and ministry, strengthened him during his suffering on the cross, and played vital role in his resurrection. And before Jesus ascended to his father, he promised to send the Holy Spirit as a permanent replacement of himself on earth, till his return for the church.

The Holy Spirit was expressly available to the early disciples, as he was with Jesus. But he now resides in all post-Pentecost disciples as he indwelled Jesus during his time on earth. By this new role, he has become more significant in Jesus' disciples through supernatural manifestations in their lives.

Even before his full manifestation on the day of Pentecost, many disciples experienced his presence. And after the day of

Pentecost, others received his power. Stephen was filled with the Holy Spirit as he lay dying after he was stoned by his persecutors.

The apostle Paul also experienced him on the way to Damascus to go and persecute believers in the faith.

> *"And Jesus being full of the Holy Ghost returned from Jordan, and was led by the Spirit into the wilderness" (Luke 4: 1).*

> *"But he, being full of the Holy Ghost, looked up stedfastly into heaven, and saw the glory of God, and Jesus standing on the right hand of God, And said, Behold, I see the heavens opened, and the Son of man standing on the right hand of God" (Acts 7: 55-56)*

It is not really possible to reach a fair conclusion on the reality of the Holy Spirit without an unbiased, honest, and genuine theological survey of the Bible. It is only in the light of God's word that the concept of the Holy Spirit can be properly reviewed and understood.

This is because, concepts such as The Holy Spirit, the divine Trinity, salvation, redemption, and many other sacred doctrines of their nature are matters of faith. For this reason, they cannot be effectively explained by only academic appraisals.

However, it is important that they are correctly explained so that they are not mis-understood. Quoting the apostle Paul, he said,

> *"But I certify you, brethren, that the gospel which was preached of me is not after man. For I neither received it of man, neither was I*

taught it, but by the revelation of Jesus Christ"
(Galatians 1: 11-12).

So, except God reveals himself, no one can understand him. Receiving knowledge of supernatural secrets can only be by the grace of God. And the hunger for such knowledge increases as a person keeps a closer walk with him, as facilitated by his Spirit. For It is by the revelation of God, not by the theories of science or human models of philosophy, that the knowledge of the Holy Spirit can be received. That is why the Bible is still the best place to find him.

"In that hour Jesus rejoiced in spirit, and said, I thank thee, O Father, Lord of heaven and earth, that thou hast hid these things from the wise and prudent, and hast revealed them unto babes: even so, Father; for so it seemed good in thy sight" (Luke 10: 21).

It is from this perspective that the reader must proceed in the journey to finding and knowing the Holy Spirit. If man will rely on the GPS (Global Positioning System) for perfect direction in human journey, those in search for God's truth will not be misguided as they follow the leading of his Spirit.

The Holy Spirit is an intercessor who prays for children of God and teaches them the truth about Christ. He is the divine channel through whom Christians are endued with the power and given responsibilities of taking the saving message of the gospel into the dark places of this earth. (Acts 16: 6-7)

He inspired the parchment-writings of Old Testament prophets and enabled New Testament apostles to do exploits for God's kingdom. It was by his motivation that ordinary, illiterate fishermen became fearless teachers, preachers and church planters in dangerous mission fields, just as his supernatural voice gave them instructions.

Jews and Gentiles alike, men, women, young and old, all risked their lives, not minding persecutions, oppressions, threats, imprisonment, hardships and even death, as they went wherever the Spirit led them in order to save perishing souls for the kingdom of God.

The Holy Spirit was Moses' light-house when he led the children of Israel during their wilderness experience. He was before them by day as a pillar of cloud and by night as a pillar of fire. And whenever he stood behind them, he was light to them, but darkness to their enemies.

He empowered Samson with strength, incubated Daniel with wisdom, and anointed David for leadership. He worked with Jesus throughout his earthly life, baptized the early disciples with gifts for ministry on the day of Pentecost, and is the same person and power indwelling and baptizing Christians in this present age.

The Holy Spirit is a vital part of every Christian's victorious life and a spiritual mentor who patiently guides believers in the way of Christ. He is the one who directs their footsteps, teaching them everything they need to know about walking with God and working for him (John 14: 26).

To encounter the Holy Spirit is to experience the cleansing power of divine fire. This holy-fire prepares surrendered souls for the challenges of sacrificial service. A person who encounters him, experiences the incredible power of Christ's resurrection and acquires the passion to love like Christ.

Through his indwelling presence, God prepares Christians in every area of life, making them become more like Jesus in their thought, word, deed. He carefully and patiently prunes believers until they can bear Christ-like fruit in a world that has become barren due to sin.

The prompting of the Holy Spirit initiates the search for Christ in a reprobate soul. He makes a person hungry for God's word in ways that are extra-ordinary. And "Holy fire" that results in zeal for service in the kingdom of God can only come through his baptism.

He offers help to weary souls just like Jesus offered streams of living water to thirsty souls. And he gives divine gifts to those who diligently seek God. He guides all people of faith, protecting them from the challenges of the wicked and strengthens them in times of temptation.

This Holy Spirit is "the promise of the Father" spoken of by the prophets. While he operated silently in the Old Testament, he came to full manifestation in the New Testament dispensation through the out-pouring of his power upon the early Church. This unprecedented act occurred on that first Pentecost after Christ's ascension into heaven.

The Holy Spirit is a supernatural Being. He is a spirit being that has a mind, a will and expresses emotions. Though he came from God the Father, he works as an equal partner with him, just as he does with Jesus Christ who is the other divine member of the holy Trinity

"Let this mind be in you, which was also in Christ Jesus: Who, being in the form of God, thought it not robbery to be equal with God" (Philippians 2:5-6).

The title, Holy Spirit, rightly describes him for he is a spirit in the semblance of the Holy God. By his nature, he cannot be seen with the ordinary human eye, though his supernatural presence can be felt in the different forms through which he manifests in the lives of believers and in the church.

"Even the Spirit of truth; whom the world cannot receive, because it seeth him not, neither knoweth him: but ye know him; for he dwelleth with you, and shall be in you" (John 14:17).

Because the Holy Spirit is a person, he has a soul. As a result, he expresses emotions like joy, peace, and love. But he can also grieve and be grieved. He is the divine power that establishes order, and as a result, he does not tolerate confusion, mummering, rebellion, or disorderliness or whatever habits that lead to these vices.

He is addressed with the title "Holy", which term is reserved entirely for deity, people of perfect knowledge or enlightenment, sacred temples or places of worship due to the purity of their character. By these qualifications, the Holy Spirit, who is worthy of complete devotion qualifies for the title.

The Holy Spirit is the vessel through whom God reveals his mind, in part, to Christians and executes his plans in the church. He is the life-giving spirit through whom God calls all things into spiritual or physical reality. He was a very active participant in the six-day creation project that produced the universe and all that is in it.

He was the power by whom God moved upon the face of the waters when the newly created earth was yet without form and void, and darkness was upon the face of the deep. He is God's breath that turned the life-less body of the created man into a living being.

"And the Lord God formed man of the dust of the ground, and breathed into his nostrils the breath of life; and man became a living soul" (Genesis 2: 7).

Unfortunately, most people of faith, even in this New Testament dispensation, do not appreciate the roles which the Holy Spirit plays to make their lives better. As a result, he is constantly and unconsciously relegated to the background on matters that require spiritual attention.

In the prayer lives of most believers, as well as in general relationship with the sovereign deity, the Holy Spirit is the least mentioned. And the result is that many Christians unconsciously defraud themselves of the numerous privileges and benefits of this generous source of supernatural gifts.

He is the source of that supernatural power in Christians which enable them to excel in areas where they least imagined any success. He blesses children of God with transformational, spiritual abilities that enable the ordinary, natural person to accomplish extra-ordinary feats.

The Holy Spirit is not an angel as some imagine or like the invisible image of any other created being. He is a divine person in the likeness of God the Father or God the Son. He hears, sees, speaks, feels, and is Omni-present, Omni-scent, and Omni-potent.

He has perfect knowledge of all human thoughts, imaginations, and presumptive actions. And every intent of the human mind is open to him as nothing can be hidden from him. He is the intercessors vital partner and the prayer-warrior's guide, helping them to pray according to the will of God.

> *"For there is not a word in my tongue, but, lo, O Lord, thou knowest it altogether. Thou hast beset me behind and before, and laid thine hand upon me. Such knowledge is too wonderful for me; it is high, I cannot attain unto it" (Psalms 139:4-6.)*

"I the Lord search the heart, I try the reins, even to give every man according to his ways, and according to the fruit of his doings" (Jeremiah 17: 10).

Spiritual truths are usually not easily understood. But with the help of the Holy Spirit, the mind of a Christian is guided beyond mere rational reasoning to discover and operate at deeper dimensions of faith, wisdom, knowledge and understanding. This is that level where the mysteries reserved for those who love God are revealed.

The spirit of a man only comprehends carnal things. Its capacity to know is limited to certain depths of understanding in arts and science. But when the Spirit of God is involved, the human mind is enabled above the natural capacity to the level where it can access spiritual truths.

The new life in Christ is not a guarantee against physical and spiritual challenges. But the faithful Christian is assured of the consoling comfort of the Holy Spirit when anxieties, fear, and emotional distresses arise. He is the one who shows up in those moments of desolation with soothing joy, easing hurts, relieving grief and assuaging any anguish.

He is the Spirit of truth who ceaselessly bears witness that Christ is the way, the truth, and the life. Any Christian who abides by his counsel, consistently following his guidance and leading, will not succumb to evil attractions or miss their direction in the journey of life.

When he convinces a person that sin is evil, he calls that soul into repentance and encourages him to live by the righteous standard of God. This way, he shapes lives for God's kingdom, enabling Christians to overcome worldly seductions. He then uses these transformed lives as shinning-light in a dark and perishing world.

The Holy Spirit leads believers in the way that helps them avoid conflict with divine principles. He renews the right spiritual attitude within human souls, so they do not falter and gives God's children the boldness to overcome carnal as well as spiritual challenges.

The presence of the holy Spirit in a human life makes a huge difference in his character. In Caesarea Philippi, for instance, he showed through the life of a Roman centurion how simple acts of righteous devotion, humility, kindness and generosity can attract divine attention.

The illustration in the Bible is given about a man called Cornelius. He was a kind man who always showed compassion to God's chosen people. Eventually, this god-fearing gentile received divine recognition that earned him permanent mention in biblical narrative (Acts 10: 1-3).

The Holy Spirit can search out every human intention. He perceives everyone's thoughts, whether they be good or bad and knows the imagination of every mind. He understands all works of men and cannot be confused, duped or manipulated by the natural man. And not even the angels or any spirit beings can deceive him.

It is by his conviction that the gift of believing-faith comes alive. And through his inspiration, human beliefs become real and grow strong. He is the divine character that motivates the habits of obedience, commitment, humility, and awe in every man. For this reason, the psalmist observed:

"When I consider the heavens, the work of thy fingers, the moon and the stars, which thou hast ordained; What is man, that thou art mindful

of him? and the son of man, that thou visitest him. for thou hast made him a little lower than angels, and has crowned him with glory and honour. Thou madest him to have dominion over the works of thy hands; thou hast put all things under his feet" (Psalms 8: 3-6).

The powerful lights in the firmament, the birds flying in the sky, the beasts of the forests, the sheep of the fields, the mountains and valleys, and the abundance of the seas, the dew, wind, dust, and the other elements, are all the excellent works of the divine Trinity.

And when you add these up to the amazing design of the universe, and consider the finest detail by which everything works, the day and night in their sequence, the summer, autumn, winter, and spring in their seasons, the wind, the darkness, and the sunshine, you will marvel. And you will no-longer doubt the presence of the Holy Spirit, who the creator of the universe acknowledged as his co-designer.

PRAYER POINTS

1). Holy Spirit of the living God, have your way in my life, in Jesus name.

2). Bright and morning star, lead me in the right path, in Jesus name.

3). Spirit of the living God, revive my life with your fire, in Jesus name.

4). Excellent Spirit of the Father, reveal God's mind to my heart, in Jesus name.

5). Spirit of truth, give me knowledge from above, in Jesus name.

6). Comforter from God, let me experience you, in Jesus name.

7). Holy Spirit, make me to rejoice in the knowledge of your truth, in Jesus name.

8). Life-giving Breath of God, thank you for keeping me alive, in Jesus name.

9). Holy Spirit, I thank you for turning me from an ordinary thing into and extra-ordinary person, in Jesus name.

10). O God that searches the heart, grant me my heart's desire, in Jesus name.

11). Holy Teacher, teach me God's ways, in Jesus name.

12). Holy Spirit, let your presence in my life make me unique, in Jesus name.

13). Spirit of God, help me to love like Christ, in Jesus name.

14). Holy Spirit, refine my thoughts and imaginations, in Jesus name.

FOUR

Concept of the Holy Trinity

One of the five major doctrines of the Christian faith is the belief in the Holy Trinity. That is the belief in the existence of three persons in the form of God the Father, God the Son and God the Holy Spirit, as one God. And while this concept is not specifically so mentioned in the Bible, the obvious operations of these three-in-one persons, as variously stated by scriptures, are very difficult to undermine, even by its critics.

An un-biased study of the Bible will reveal unexplainable events that allude to the cooperative work of respective persons of the divine trinity. And numerous other supernatural acts in the Bible show a divine, tripartite function that back-up the claim of a Holy Trinity in operation. So, a good understanding of this concept is needful in order not to mix it up with poly theism.

The doctrine of the Trinity teaches that there is One Sovereign God. But it further explains that according to Christian beliefs, there are three eternal persons, in the form of God the Father, God the Son, and God the Holy Spirit, represented in this one God. All of these three divine persons are spiritual in nature, are equal in power and character, and proceed from the same source.

In comparison with human models of philosophy, the three persons of the Christian faith would be referred to as three gods. And for this reason, several people even in the Christian community, struggle with accepting this seemingly-complex, concept which they cannot easily explain.

So, while some people readily acknowledge the idea of God, as Father and creator of the universe and all things, others, especially those outside the family of the Christian faith, contest the claim of Jesus as "God the son", and the Holy Spirit "as God", also.

But, like most issues of faith, the doctrine of the Trinity is a mystery that is beyond the comprehension of the natural mind or academic knowledge. It does not agree with any extrapolations of logic and will not fit into classical philosophical models. So, in these quarters, the concept of the Trinity is regarded as absurd and only self-contradictory.

However, many scriptures literally leaping out of the Bible, readily confirm the reality of this pillar of the Christian faith. Thus, while acknowledging the uniqueness of the persons of the divine Trinity, in terms of their respective sacred obligations, the scriptures confirm their obvious equality in authority, character and unity in operation.

The natural human environment limits the human mind to certain levels of knowledge and understanding, especially to the things that are easily perceptible. But as the mind acquires higher levels of knowledge, it begins to appreciate hidden things that were formerly thought to be mysteries.

Understanding the concept of the Holy Trinity is the unraveling of one mystery. This mystery is a truth which those who only reason on the human level of knowledge consider as impossibility. But their failure to acknowledge this truth will not make it a lie.

From the activities of the Holy Trinity in the Old Testament, the reader will find an overwhelming corporeality of the Father, Son and Holy Spirit. Also, the operation of the Father, the Son and the Holy Spirit in the New Testament dispensation, as three distinct persons, yet in one entity, will leave the Bible student with no doubt that the Trinity is a concept of unprecedented reality.

This concept really exists as the scriptures say and each of the three distinct persons is truly God. It is the only one such divinely conceived model of its kind in nature. Human religion cannot recreate it, neither can science or philosophy replicate it. This is because its origin is divine, and it proceeds supernaturally from domains that are beyond human perception.

This statement is not in condemnation of the principle underling the pursuit for human knowledge but only buttresses the truth that the Supreme Deity, in his nature, cannot be fully understood or meaningful comprehended except by those who are minded to searching beyond the natural dimension of human knowledge.

It is true that the concept of the divine Trinity sounds complex. But it is the biased, human evaluation of this truth that made it look so complicated. That is why, in the words of the Apostle Paul, Christians are advised to:

> *"Beware lest any man spoil you through philosophy and vain deceit, after the tradition of men, after the rudiments of the world, and not after Christ" (Colossians 2: 8).*

Christian doctrines are founded on the premise of God's word, and based on his commandments, laws, statutes, all of which proceed from a supernatural source. So, it is only expected that the knowledge, understanding and application of them must follow protocols which quite often involve divine intervention.

Sacred doctrines in the model of Holy Trinity are spiritual in origin. As a result, they never make sense to the ordinary human mind. But it makes a whole lot of difference to people with a spiritual mind-set, whose souls are filled with holy desires for righteous purposes. In the words of A. W Tozer, "they are matters set aside for genuine possessors of faith, and not for professors of faith".

God's ways are higher and greater than any human ways, means or methods can explain. That is why human approaches of classical philosophy, have been un-successful in explaining the divine nature of God. Comprehension of the divine nature of God cannot be obtained through philosophical theories, mere academic brainstorming or captured inside a scientific test-tube.

But in his goodness, he sometimes grants the natural mind a peek into his own mind (through the lenses of the Holy Spirit), to enable the ordinary man to understand his nature, will and character. This happens when the cravings for spiritual things, supersede the inordinate hunger for logic.

It is in this glorious condition that God manifests through his Spirit to reveal himself in supernatural ways to the natural man. Supernatural mysteries, which include deep knowledge and wisdom proceed from God. And because they are spiritual in origin, they are reserved for chosen children of God whose minds are set on spiritual things. These hidden things belong to God and he unveils them to the world through his chosen vessels.

"He made known his ways unto Moses, his acts unto the children of Israel" (Psalm 103: 7).

No one knows the mind of God, except his Spirit. It is God's Spirit that reveals his will to his children at the appropriate time and place. Through this process, the natural man obtains insight into divine matters. And just as no one else but God's Spirit can reveal him to humanity, no measure of intellectual effort or exercise in human scholarship can define his nature beyond what is stated in his word.

People who view the doctrine of Holy Trinity without considering the numerous, joint-acts of the Father, Son and Holy Spirit or who over-look the scriptural inferences to this unique concept in the Bible, will be trapped in the academic net of theoretical scholarship. For the secrets of God can only be unveiled by his Spirit to those who are honest seekers of knowledge. Such people are un-biased in spirit and soul.

> *"The secret things belong unto the Lord our God: but those things which are revealed belong unto us and to our children forever, that we may do all the words of this law"* *(Deuteronomy 29:29).*

The concept of the divine Trinity is not poly-theism. This is because poly theism is the title under which rational thinkers categorize its seeming equivalents. For reasons already explained above, the concept of the divine Trinity will not fit into this broad spectrum of human philosophy whose ideas are based on rational thinking.

From the argument of non-Christian philosophers, the idea of a "Trinity of God's" perfectly fits their theory of non-contradiction which is also known as the law of contradiction. In logic, the law of contradiction states that contradictory propositions cannot be true in the same sense at the same time. That is to say, we cannot agree in one sense that the belief in multiple gods is polytheism while arguing on the same basis that belief in the Trinity is not.

Well, there cannot be any contradiction here if only we understand that the two concepts differ in nature and origin. For while the idea of polytheism is of human creation, the concept of the Trinity originated from God. It is unique in itself, has no equivalents and is unprecedented in nature. It is neither a religious idea that evolved out of the belief systems of ancient cultures, nor a sacred opinion deduced from mere philosophical theories of man. It is God's own idea and is clearly supported by his word.

From human experience, we observe that the mind is imperfect and limited to what it can what it can know. That is the reason honest engineers are not utterly surprised when air planes designed by the principles of aerodynamism, eventually crash or when ships sink in the ocean, trains derail in their tracks and automobile brakes fail when a vehicle is in motion. Yet the earth that God created and hung upon nothing remains perfectly in place. It has never tilted or spurn out of place. This is because, the word of God is the only reliable witness for itself.

Scientific theories and philosophical concepts may change with time, but the ageless word of God remains the same. So, it is as a person encounters the Holy Spirit, who is reserved mainly for those who desire or have tasted the miracle of salvation, that understanding the concept of the Holy Trinity, becomes easy.

Without this knowledge, people will continue to toy with the opinion that the existence of three distinct spiritual personalities as one God, is impossible. But the word of God remains eternally credible concerning this subject matter as in other complex issues in the Bible. And numerous scriptural references confirm the joint roles of the Father, Son, and the Holy Spirit, make the concept of the Holy Spirit even more credible.

Through several Old and New testament scriptures, the bible speaks eloquently about the person of God's Spirit. This is God's vessel for transforming lives, spreading his gospel, working signs and wonders, and kindling spiritual fire of revival within the church.

It will be un-imaginable what the universe would look like if God did not exist from the timeless beginning in the very form, personalities, or dimensions he stated in his word. These are the very dimensions by which the heaven, the earth, and all things that exist were formed.

The Holy Spirit Is first encountered in the opening verses of Genesis chapter one, where the scripture says,

"In the beginning God created the heaven and the earth. And the earth was without form, and void; and darkness was upon the face of the deep" (Genesis 1: 1-2).

At this stage, the earth that God created was in total disorder. This was its un-wholesome condition until "the Spirit of God" moved upon the face of the waters. Thereafter, God called the light into being, then separated it from the darkness. He then created a firmament that divided the waters above, from the body of the waters below. He called this firmament, heaven.

Furthermore, God commanded the waters under the heaven to be gathered in one place and commanded the dry land to come out of the waters. And he called this dry land, earth

In this orderly sequence, God commanded the earth to bring forth grass, the herb that yields seed, and fruit tree that yields fruit according to its kind, "whose seed is in itself".

Then God called forth the great lights, and galaxies, and set them above in the firmament to give light to the earth. He commanded the greater light to rule over the day, the lesser light to rule the night and to separate the light from the darkness.

He then filled the waters with an abundance of sea-creatures, before calling the birds that fly in the firmament above into being. Thereafter, he caused the earth to bring forth the beast, the cattle, and creeping things which he made, according to their kind.

Finally, he turned to his partners in creation, and said, "Let Us make man in Our image, according to our likeness. This is another tacit evidence that God worked all along with some silent partners in the great creation project that produced the very things that gave this universe its form and character.

So, from the creation narrative, one begins to find some of the numerous threads of indisputable evidence that support the existence of the Trinity. In these scriptures, the respective identities of each divine person begin to be unveiled.

Thus, the remarkable roles played by the silent, yet active persons of the Holy Spirit and the Word (Jesus), not just in conceiving the complex plan of the universe, but in rolling out of its entire master plan, cannot be understated. And from these opening verses of the book of Genesis to the last verse of the book of Revelation, we find more scriptures that point to the great concept known as the Holy Trinity.

> *"In the beginning God created the heaven and the earth. And the earth was without form, and void; and darkness was upon the of the deep. And the Spirit of God moved upon the face of the waters. And God said: let there be light, and there was light (Genesis 1:1-3).*

In this opening Old Testament narrative of the book of Genesis, the bible identified two persons involved the work of creation. One is simply described as God, and the other, the Spirit of God. It was not until the books of the prophets, that the second person of the trinity (God the Son) is mentioned. Before then, he was only described in several places as the Word.

Further evidences of God existing in three forms as God the Father, God the Son and God the Holy Spirit are found, not only in the books of Moses, but also in book of the prophets, in the Gospels and Epistles in the Bible. Some include:

> *"Then the Lord said, "Behold, the man has become like one of Us, to know good and evil: and now, lest he put forth his hand, and take*

also of the tree of life, and eat, and live forever Therefore the Lord God sent him forth from the garden of Eden, to till the ground from whence he was taken" (Genesis 3: 22-23).

"In the beginning was the Word, and the Word was with God, and the Word was God. The same was in the beginning with God" (John 1: 1-2).

"Let this mind be in you, which was also in Christ Jesus: Who, being in the form of God, thought it not robbery to be equal with God: (Philippians 2: 5-6)

When some Old Testament scriptures on the divine trinity are critically compared to their New Testament parallels, a mystery is un-raveled. This secret shows that the creation process was specifically handled by all the members of the divine Trinity, and not just by God the Father alone, as some erroneously think.

From the Hebrew context, the title "Elohim" is the name frequently used to describe God. And in Genesis chapter one verse one, the title Elohim, applied to God is used in the masculine, plural noun form. This is consistent with the claim that more than one entity was present in the creation project.

These and other scriptures eliminate the idea that it was angels that assisted in this exercise, as some scholars assert. Angels are not equivalent to God. And when God created man, he said, *"let us make man in our image, after our likeness" (Genesis 1: 26).* Notice that the man God created was not in the semblance and character of angels, but in the image and likeness of himself, and his divine partners, all of whose unique nature differ from those angels and other created forms.

"And God said, let Us make man in our image, after our likeness: and let them have dominion over the fish of the sea, and over the foul of the air, and over the cattle, and over all the earth, and over every creeping thing that creepeth upon the earth (Genesis 1: 26)".

Thus, through this open-minded approach to the word of God, we see how less cumbersome it is to find one of the most complex concepts of Christian faith simply explained. Beyond these, there are even more evidences in the Bible pointing to the truth that God the Father, God the Son, and God the Holy Spirit, always existed as one entity from ageless eternity and have co-operated in unity from then.

In the first verse of the first chapter of the Gospel of Saint John, to whom the mystery of the Trinity was also revealed, this Apostle points out that Christ is the person of the god-head whom the Bible refers to as the "Word". So too does prophet Moses imply in the book of Genesis chapter one, and verse one.

Thus, while Jesus was not specifically identified by name in the opening chapter of the book of Genesis, latter record of events as well as subsequent scriptures undoubtedly confirm that he is the spoken Word mentioned in every manifestation of the Triune deity.

To Hebrew theologians and ancient philosophers however, "The Word" typified various things. To the psalmist for instance, the word was an agent of creation (Psalm 33:6). It represented God's law and symbolized his standard of holiness (Psalms 119: 11). To the prophets, it was indicative of the source of divine message (Hosea 1: 2) and in Greek philosophy, it implied divine essence. So, apostle John's illustration of Jesus as the "Word", is only consistent with the scripture in Genesis chapter one and verse one and in other places in the Bible (John 1: 14).

Also, in the event of Jesus' baptism, we find another corporate involvement of the three persons of the divine Trinity. On that day of Jesus' (God the Son) baptism, God the Holy Spirit manifests as a dove to confirm his deity, while God the Father testifies of his Son-ship.

> *"And Jesus, when he was baptized, went up straightway out of the water; and, lo, the heavens were opened unto him, and he saw the Spirit of God descending like a dove, and lighting upon him; And lo a voice from heaven, saying, This is my beloved Son, in whom I am well pleased" (Matthew 3: 16-17).*

So, while the word Trinity is not explicitly stated in the bible, its concept is too prominent to be ignored, its significance too obvious to go un-recognized, and the respective roles the individual entities play in unity, quite invaluable to be disregarded.

It is on the divine premise of this unity in divinity, that the foundation of the Christian faith is spiritually founded. No one has seen God to be capable of disputing the form which he revealed is his nature. For this reason, several bible scholars agree on the concept of the Holy Trinity.

From philosophical perspective, such a claim will be considered a paradox. But when you call into mind that issues of divine dimension rest completely upon the infallible word of God, it becomes reasonable not to rely solely on scientific theories, human logic or reason in addressing the matter of the Holy Spirit.

Some of the grounds for which the concept of the divine Trinity is corroborated by several infallible truths, abound in both the Old Testament scriptures as well as in the New Testament gospels, epistles, and in Revelations. (Deuteronomy 6: 4; Isaiah 44:6 John 10: 30).

These and other scriptures that support the existence of the divine Trinity can be found in the underlisted books of the Bible:

1). *Matthew 28: 19-20.*

"Go ye therefore, and teach all nations, baptizing them in the name of the Father, and of the Son, and the Holy Ghost: Teaching them to observe all things whatsoever I have commanded you; and lo, I am with you always, even unto the end of the world, Amen"

2). *John 15: 26-27*

"But when the Comforter is come, whom I will send unto you from the Father, even the Spirit of truth, which proceedeth from the Father, he shall testify of me: And ye also shall bear witness, because ye have been with me from the beginning".

3). *1 Corinthians 12: 4-6*

"Now there are diversities of gifts, but the same Spirit. And there are differences of administrations, but the same Lord. And there are diversities of operations, but it is the same God which worketh all in all".

4). *2 Corinthians 13: 14.*

"The grace of the Lord Jesus Christ, and the love of God, and the communion of the Holy Ghost, be with you all".

5). *Ephesians 2: 18-22.*

"For through him we both access by one Spirit unto the Father. Now therefore ye are no more strangers and foreigners, but fellow citizens with the saints, and of the household of God; and are built upon the foundation of the apostles and

prophets, Jesus Christ himself being the chief corner stone; In whom all the building fitly framed together growth unto an holy temple in the Lord: In whom ye also are builded together for an habitation of God through the Spirit".

6). *1 Thessalonians 1: 2-5.*

"We give thanks to God always for you all, making mention of you in our prayers; Remembering without ceasing your work of faith, and labour of love, and patience of hope in our Lord Jesus Christ, in the sight of God and our Father; Knowing, brethren beloved, your election of God".

7). *1 Peter 1: 2.*

"Elect according to the foreknowledge of God the Father, through sanctification of the Spirit, unto obedience and sprinkling of the blood of Jesus Christ: Grace unto you, and peace, be multiplied".

In some of these scriptures, mention is made of God the Father, God the Holy Spirit, and God the Son. Here, special recognition is given respectively to the three members of the Holy Trinity for their joint effort in the great work of redemption and not in order of position, eminence or power.

Thus, the victory of God's plan of redemption, which was executed by his Son's humble surrender at the cross and sustained by the work of his Holy Spirit at Christ's resurrection, is convincing evidence of the mystery of the doctrine of the Holy Trinity.

The Holy Trinity is about God's divine family. All three persons of the divine deity are spirit Beings. They are not just equivalent but equal in nature, and character. They are divine members of the god-head and not some abstract, imaginary deities as some believe, or say.

Finally, if anyone is still in doubt about the idea of the Trinity, I believe the apostle Paul's invocation of the three members of the god-head, "the Father, the Son, and the Holy Spirit", in his farewell blessing to the believers in Corinth, will lay this matter to rest. In that scripture that is now used as doxology in many churches, he prays like this,

> *"The grace of the Lord Jesus Christ, and the love*
> *of God, and the communion of the Holy Ghost,*
> *be with you all. Amen (2 Corinthians 13: 14).*

A scripture like the one above, which makes specific reference to the tri-unity of the god-head undeniably confirms the nature of the Sovereign Deity, as three eternal persons of equal divine essence and character, who exist as one indivisible God.

Therefore, to say that the Spirit of God is equally God, as the scriptures declare, is incontrovertible. To believe that each divine person is equal to the other in character and essence, according to the Bible, is theologically indisputable. And to maintain, in line with God's word that the Father, the Son and the Holy Spirit exist as one, is unquestionably true.

The Holy Spirit is an incredible teacher who inspires and reveals secret knowledge. He is the sacred vessel that God uses to convict souls for Christ, coverts them, brings eternal joy to those converts and guarantees them everlasting peace. Through his operation in the lives of converts, they receive divine amazing grace, which connects human souls to the heart of the Father. And he belongs to the family of the Holy Trinity.

PRAYER PIONTS

1). Father, Son and Holy Spirit, make your ways known to me, in Jesus name.

2). My Father, even in my uniqueness, teach me to be humble, in Jesus name.

3). Holy Spirit, protect my mind from pollution by evil knowledge, in Jesus name

4). O God, use me to make effective disciples for your kingdom, in Jesus name.

5). Holy Spirit, inspire me to act like Jesus that I may please the Father, in Jesus name.

6). Father, Son and Holy Spirit, I thank you because you are not like the gods of my ancestors, in Jesus name.

7). O God, I thank you for the unity in the divine Trinity, in Jesus name.

8). Thank you Father, Son and Holy Spirit, because you know all things, in Jesus name.

9). Father, Son and Holy Spirit, I honor you because you are supreme in power, in Jesus name.

10). Holy Spirit, I thank you for making me know that I am not God even though I have his image, in Jesus name.

11). O God, I thank you for the testimony of your Son through the Holy Spirit, in Jesus name.

12). Holy Spirt, teach me to observe what Jesus commanded about God, in Jesus name.

13). Holy Spirit, help me with regular access to God through his Son, in Jesus name.

14). Thank you God for your grace through the fellowship with your Son and the Holy Spirit, in Jesus name.

CHAPTER

The Holy Spirit
(In the Old
and New Testaments.)

In the old Testament.

The third person of the god-head was rarely referred to by the title of the Holy Spirit during the Old Testament era. Only once in the psalms and in the book of Prophet Isaiah, was he called the Holy Spirit. Even though he was present all the while, most Old Testament scriptures and characters referred to him by the title, "Spirit of God".

> *"In the beginning God created the heaven and the earth. And the earth was without form, and void; and darkness was upon the face of the deep. And the Spirit of God moved upon the face of the waters" (Genesis 1:1-2)*

> *"Cast me not away from thy presence; and take not thy holy spirit from me" (Psalms 51:11).*

*"But they rebelled, and vexed his holy Spirit:
therefore he was turned to be their enemy, and
he fought against them. Then he remembered
the days of old, Moses, and his people, saying,
Where is he that brought them up out of the
sea with the shepherd of his flock? where is he
that put his holy Spirit within him" (Isaiah
63: 10-11).*

For the most part of the Old Testament period, the person of the Holy Spirit was given very little attention, as if he did not matter or exist. But the era of the prophets was different. They could not be silent about him because it was through his concealed presence that they all divinely operated.

During that epoch, he was inconspicuous yet expressly accessible to the prophets, Judges, Priests and Kings. For this reason, the sacred offices occupied by certain dignitaries in ancient Hebrew societies were highly revered. Such chosen persons were the avenues through whom God's word, his law, commandments, statutes, judgments, and testimonies were passed to his children, as the Spirit gave them revelation, vision, or utterance.

The birth of Jesus, his death, resurrection, and ascension into heaven, were some of the activities that signaled the beginning of the New Testament. Before then, the Holy Spirit did not have a permanent relationship with people of faith as he came to be after the day of Pentecost.

In the Old Testament period, he came upon God's chosen vessels as the occasion demanded, filled them for certain assignments, empowered them for specific purposes and departed. Great Bible characters like Bezalel, Oholiab, Sampson, and King Saul are examples of some people he used in this manner.

King David was honorably testified of by God as a man after

his heart. Yet when he sinned in the matter of Beersheba, he feared that God would take his Holy Spirit from him. This was because he knew the consequences of a life completely bereft of the Holy Spirit. (Psalm 51: 11).

The Spirit of God operated in several forms in the Old Testament era that may sound alien to the post-Pentecost student of the Bible. While his operation then was insignificant, he still expressed himself in tangible forms that described his character or defined his nature. Some of these forms include:

1). **The Spirit of God.**

In the ancient Hebrew language, the phrase, "Spirit of God" is referred to as "Ruach Ha-Kodesh". This term rightly conveys the same meaning for wind, spirit and breath respectively. This is the first name by which the Holy Spirit was recognized in the Bible. The apostle Paul used this same title which is found in the book of Genesis, to describe the Holy Spirit in the body of his first letter to the believers in Corinth. (Genesis 1: 1-2; 1 Corinthians 3: 16; 6: 19).

In the Old Testament, the scriptures reveal how a slave-boy called Joseph was divinely promoted from the Egyptian prison to the palace of Pharaoh. This act, the Bible states, was only because, as Pharaoh testified, "the Spirit of God was in him". By the help of this Spirit. This Joseph interpreted the Pharaohs' dream (Genesis 41: 38).

By the same Spirit of God as he was known, God called Bezaleel the son of Uri, of the tribe of Judah and Aholiab, the son of Ahisamach, of the tribe of Dan, both of whom he filled in wisdom, understanding and skill to design the furniture, curtains and priestly garments for ministry in the ancient Tabernacle (Exodus 35: 30- 35).

2). **Audible voice.**

The Old Testament characters described the Holy Spirit as the audible voice of God. Men and women of old, from Adam, Noah, Abraham, Moses to the prophets, and kings heard his voice clearly. He still speaks today, as softly and audibly, as he did in the past. (Genesis 12: 1; Exodus 3: 1-4; 1 Kings 19: 11)

3). **Fiery oven/Firepot.**

In the narrative describing God's initial covenant with Abraham, the Holy Ghost was portrayed as an oven. He was the smoking furnace and burning lamp that consumed the offering presented by Abraham. (Genesis 15: 17; Psalms 21: 9)

4). **Flames of fire.**

During the Old Testament epoch, the Holy Spirit appeared in various forms on different occasions. One of these forms was as flaming fire. It was from the midst of the burning bush that "God the Holy Spirit" spoke to Moses (Exodus 3: 2-5).

5). **Pillar of cloud, and Pillar of fire.**

The Holy Spirit appeared as pillars of cloud and fire in ancient times. These were some of the physical forms by which he revealed himself to the children of God. As pillar of cloud by day and pillar of fire by night, he led the children of Israel along the way, during their wilderness journey.

He went ahead of them in a pillar of cloud by day to lead them in the way he wanted them to go and as a pillar of fire by night to give them light. This enabled them to travel by day and night.

And when the pillar of cloud stood behind the children of

Israel, it was as thick darkness to separate them from their enemies (Exodus 13: 21-22; 14: 19-20; Numbers 9: 19).

6). **Finger of God (psalms 8: 3)**

The finger of God represents divine power. Pharaoh's magicians attributed the supremacy of Moses' miracles over their enchantments, magic and divination, to the intervention of "The finger of God" (Exodus 8: 19).

ii). The Bible describes the "finger of God" as the instrument by which God passes instructions to his servants. God wrote the law with his finger on tablets of stone that he asked Moses to prepare Exodus 31: 18)

iii). The "finger of God" exposes sin and reveals human depravity. In that case, it becomes an instrument of wrathful appointment and judgment against a person, congregation or nation who disobey God. In the kingdom of Babylon, God scribbled his judgment on the royal walls of King Belshazzar's palace (Daniel 5: 5,24).

This was because, King Belshazzar drank from the sacred vessels of gold and silver which his father, Nebuchadnezzar, had taken from the temple in Jerusalem. This foolish act was a reproach of the Sovereign God.

As the King, his lords, their wives and concubines drank wine from these sacred vessels, they praised their gods of silver, bronze, iron, wood, and stone. This outrageous act attracted the burning wrath of God. And without delay, God wrote a grievous but deserving judgment on the royal walls of the King's palace.

This happened during the Babylonian captivity of Israel where Daniel was a slave. This Daniel was described as the man in whom is "the spirit of the holy gods", perhaps in reference to the Holy Spirit. He was invited to explain the handwriting, after all the King's wise-men, magicians, soothsayers, and astrologers failed to make meaning of it.

The writing which the King saw was: Mene, Mene, Tekel, Upahsin. And by Daniel's explanation, it meant: "Mene": "God has numbered thy kingdom and finished it". "Tekel": "Thou art weighed in the balances and found wanting". And "Peres": "Thy kingdom is divided and given to the Medes and Persians". The same night that the writing was interpreted to the King by prophet Daniel, the thirty-two-year-old, proud, rebellious ruler of earthly kingdoms was slain.

Eventually, the Medes and the Persians overthrew the Babylonian empire, showing how dangerous it is to fall into the hand of a jealous God. The Holy Spirit still serves as "the finger of God". He may no longer be raising his finger against Egyptian magic or scribbling on royal walls as he did in Babylon, but he still writes on the hearts of men and women teaching them the ways of truth and justice.

7). **Shadow of God.**

Another prominent act of the Holy Spirit in the Old Testament period was the virgin conception of Mary. This was the unprecedented event that resulted in the birth of Jesus of Nazareth. (Matthew 1: 18; Luke 1:35).

This divinely orchestrated feat, generally regarded by theologians as the greatest event in bible history, was made possible by the involvement of the invisible presence of God. In the Bible, this presence is described as God's overshadowing image.

That power that overshadowed the blessed virgin Mary was none other than the presence of the Holy Spirit. He was the same Spirit of the Father that brooded over the chaotic earth and the waters at creation, before God called the light out of darkness.

By this supernatural shadow, angels, prophets, priests, kings, and servants of God in times past, received revelations, visions and dreams for the purpose reaching out to God's children. The events that occurred during the Old Testament epoch, all of which are linked to the "shadow of God", were all possible because of the powerful move of the Holy Spirit (Genesis 1: 1-2; Luke 2: 25).

Holy Spirit in the New Testament.

Relying on a litany of scriptures both in the Old and New Testaments of Bible, it is very safe to state that the person of the Holy Spirit has eternally been present, active and existed with God the Father and God the Son, in what is referred to as "eternity".

As a member of the divine god-head, it is only obvious that the Holy Spirit was present at the commencement of creation. He was the instrument through whom God the Father brought order on earth, gave life to man, and revealed his mind to prophets, kings, and priests for transmission to his children.

He played very prominent role in the holy Mary's conception of Jesus and was God's vessel that confirmed Jesus as God's Son on the day of his baptism. He strengthened Jesus during the forty-day fasting exercise preceding his earthly ministry, motivated him through life and was the sole medium responsible for his resurrection from the dead.

The Holy Spirit played eminent role in the success of Christ's earthly ministry. In apostle Peter's very effective witness for Christ to the new converts gathered in the house of Cornelius in Caesarea Philippi, he shared his personal experience of the success of Jesus' healing and deliverance activities, which he attributed to the anointing by the Holy Ghost.

"How God anointed Jesus of Nazareth with the Holy Ghost and with power: who went about doing good, and healing all that were oppressed of the devil; for God was with him"
(Acts 10: 38).

So, while the Holy Spirit may have operated from behind the scenes in the Old Testament era, his presence, power, and authority exploded into full and unrestrained manifestation during the days of Jesus ministry and the eventful feast of Pentecost after Christ's ascension.

To the ancient Hebrew, the feast of Pentecost was a major religious festival. It was a celebration of the giving of the law to Moses on Mount Sinai, which occurred fifty days after the first Passover in the wilderness. In later years, this feast attracted several devout men to Jerusalem.

On the first Pentecost after Israel came out of Egypt, three thousand children of Israel who worshipped the golden calf that Aaron made, were killed by their brothers, the Levites, on the instruction of Moses. But on the feast of Pentecost after Christ's ascension, Christ disciples were baptized in the Holy Spirit and spoke in tongues. That day, about three thousand souls were saved, baptized, and added to the church.

On the Pentecost celebrating the giving of the law to Moses, three thousand people died. But on the Pentecost after Christ's ascension, God gave the Holy Spirit to the church and three thousand people became new believers after hearing the apostle Peter preach the gospel.

This agrees with the scripture that the law (written on tablets of stones) kills. It ministers condemnation and death. But the gift of the Pentecost is ministered by the Holy Spirit. This is the spirit of grace of God, which Spirit minister's life to all who receive Jesus as Lord and Savior. (Exodus 32: 27-28; Acts 2: 41).

Since the event of that un-precedented outpouring of the Holy Spirit, his power has never ceased to move in great dimensions upon God's children. This is seen through the supernatural manifestations of his gifts upon the church, in fulfilment of God's promises.

The role of the Holy Spirit, particularly in the birth of the Early-church, is indisputable. His activity during those infant years resulted in the compilation of the gospels, the entire New Testament book titled "Acts of the Apostles" and the Epistles written by the apostles.

It will not be wrong to describe the "Acts of the Apostles" as the "Acts of the Holy Spirit". This is because it comprises an incredible collection of the sacrificial life of the early church apostles and successful works which they accomplished. For the power of God reigned over their lives during that tumultuous era of the church history.

During that dark period, identifying as a Jesus' disciple was at great risk to one's life and family. Yet these early disciples, most of whom were illiterate and of meagre economic means, daring the Roman officials, the religious leaders and the Temple authorities, defied the odds of persecution, just to spread the gospel.

Before the Holy Spirit came to indwell believers, the Bible referred to all who worked for God or walked with him including Prophets, Kings, and Priests as servants of God. This was because, the Holy Spirit used them as vessels to accomplish certain divine assignments. He did not permanently reside in them. He came upon them in measures and left at his will.

But now in Christ, all people of faith have become friends and no longer servants. The indwelling by God's Spirit in Christ's disciples and the consequent seal of adoption by the Holy Spirit whereby Christians now call God, "Abba Father", has changed all believers' status to sons and daughters, instead of servants.

The Christian of this era is comparable to a light bulb. But the Holy Spirit is the power source that causes him to glow. Without the power of the Holy Spirit, the Christian will be in perennial darkness and unable to shine. This will make the church to remain in utter obscurity as in the time when men were under Satan.

Prior to the day of Pentecost when the out-pouring of the Holy Spirit was first fully experienced, no one ever spoke in "other tongues" or operated in the gift of "Interpreting Tongues". It was the unprecedented manifestation of the Holy Spirit that triggered the uncommon experience which now distinguishes the Christians of the Apostolic age from those of the pre-Pentecost era.

So, that unique event on the day of Pentecost rightly qualifies the New Testament period to be described as the dispensation of the Holy Spirit. It marked the birth of a Holy Spirit-filled movement known as the church and represents the crowning glory of what is now known as Christianity.

> *"And, behold, I send the promise of my Father upon you: but tarry ye in the city of Jerusalem, until ye be endued with power from on high"* (Luke 24: 49).

Innumerable Christians have since re-lived the same spiritual experience enjoyed by the early disciples on that very first Pentecost. That manifestation of "Tongues and its interpretation were proof of the glorification of Jesus, and the fulfilment of his promise to the church.

So, just as in the days of the early church movement, the great potentials of the Holy Spirit are still available to all disciples today. The is because, the Holy Spirit that baptized them then, is still ready to endue honest, penitent, and committed converts with his gifts for the church, irrespective of their race, age and gender.

> *"Then Peter said unto them, Repent, and be baptized every one of you in the name of Jesus Christ for the remission of sins, and ye shall receive the gift of the Holy Ghost" (Acts 2: 38).*

Through the process of humble surrender, persistent prayer, and diligence in the word of God, any Christian can encounter the Holy Spirit and receive the benefit of his power, just as did the early disciples. Those disciples were passionate in their anticipation of God's Spirit and eventually encountered him. So too, can you.

And the more a believer lives on the "bread of life", constantly refreshing his soul, and meditating upon God's word, the more that Christian prepares himself to be filled with the glorious power, and enviable gifts of the Holy Spirit.

Some Christians argue that a believer should do nothing to receive the power of the Holy Ghost because no one deserves it. Well, scriptures clearly state there must be genuine acts of humility, repentance, followed by water baptism. These are inevitable steps that cannot be skipped.

When a sinner walks away from his transgressions, ceases from rebellious acts against God's law, ceases wickedness towards man, and deliberately turns to Christ, the Holy Spirit steps into that life and begins a transformation. The influence of the Holy Spirit upon the church is undeniable. And there is no doubt of his readiness to operate in people that believe in their hearts that Jesus is the Son of God and confess that with their mouth.

As a ready instrument of divine influence, he has always played the roles of a guiding, guarding, strengthening, preserving, and protecting agent in the lives of the righteous and the willing children of faith.

From the moment of his earliest manifestation to the disciples of Jesus in the upper room, he has been the spiritual power house behind soul-winning, spreading-wide the gospel and the incredible, miracle source working wherever Christians ministered.

Through willing New Testament believers, he has accomplished innumerable feats for the kingdom of God by unimaginable measures. No one, by his own merit, strength or personal effort can achieved in a whole life-time, what the Holy Spirit assisted person can accomplish in a moment.

The Church movement is a New Testament phenomenon borne by the divine intervention of the Holy Spirit. He is her breathe and life-blood, without whose power the Church cannot achieve anything meaningful.

He is the power that transforms the mind of a Christian, making it possible for that believer to perceive spiritual events. He is the supernatural power that collaborates with the natural mind to enable it to understand spiritual things. Illumination of the divine word, visions from heaven, and revelations given by God are all possible because of the influence of the Holy Spirit upon the Church and in the lives of Christ's faithful disciples.

Through the action of the Holy Spirit and his refining power, ordinary fishermen like Peter, Andrew, James, and John were transformed into extra-ordinary tools that turned the world upside down for Christ. He was the same divine influence that changed the life of Saul of Tarsus and turned him to the Apostle Paul.

The Holy Spirit convict's men of their sin, inspires a life of righteousness, empowers people of faith to work miracles, and enables believer's to fearlessly engage enemies of God in spiritual warfare. The devil is scared when a Christian filled with the Holy Spirit begins to minister in the name of Jesus.

Demons tremble in the presence of a Holy Ghost-filled, fire-spitting child of God. They surrender and are subdued or flee once they hear commands in the name of Jesus. This is the authority by which bondages are destroyed, evil covenants broken, curses nullified, and yokes removed.

When the Holy Spirit dwells in a person, the devil cannot harm him, wickedness will not prevail against that life, neither can demons succeed against that individual. Evil chains cannot bind such Christians, walls designed to hinder them collapse to their foundation, while doors of opportunities open to such believers on their own accord.

> *"And when they had laid many stripes upon them, they cast them into prison charging the jailor to keep them safely. Who, having received such a charge, thrust them into the inner prison, and made their feet fast in the stocks. And at midnight Paul and Silas prayed, and sang praises unto God: and the prisoners heard them. And suddenly there was a great earthquake, so that the foundations of the prison were shaken: and immediately all the doors of the prison were opened, and everyone's bands were loosed" (Acts 16: 23-26).*

The faithful prayer and fiery praises of a Holy Spirit-filled child of God always connect with heaven. That is the way they nullify the plans of the enemy. The story of apostles Paul and Silas while incarcerated in Philippi, is one good illustration here.

One day, after they delivered a young girl that brought her master means by the spirit of divination, they were arrested, stripped of their clothes beaten, and thrown into the inner dungeon. They had their feet bound in stocks as they were thrown into prison, but instead of mourning their condition, they settled for a session of violent prayer and praise. They prayed loudly and praised until the Holy Spirit came down for their rescue.

The same Holy Spirit that was available to the disciples of the early church is available for the modern-day Christian. That same power that intervened on behalf of Apostles Paul and Silas, is still effective today and shall remain the same, till Christ returns for his church.

The Holy Spirit actively cooperates with Christians in the execution of God's divine agenda. He enables believers with the spiritual resources for implementing divine purpose for the church, and in the dismantling of the works of darkness on earth. He baptizes people of faith with power to do exploits for God's kingdom, prepares and empowers believers for ministry and endues Christ's disciples with gifts through which God manifests himself to the Church.

So, it is through the activity of the Holy Spirit that the Church is blessed with supernatural gifts that promote the growth of the Church, as well as ensure outreach to the world.

The apostle Paul enumerated the spiritual gifts of the Holy Spirit in his first letter to the Church at Corinth. They are gifts that enable the ordinary person who is born-again in Christ to accomplish extra-ordinary feats to the glory of God (1 Corinthians 12: 7-11). They include:

i). **The word of Knowledge.**
ii). **The word of wisdom.**
iii). **The gift of prophecy.**
iv). **The gift of Faith.**
v). **The gifts of healing.**
vi). **The working of Miracles.**
vii). **Discerning of Spirits.**
viii). **gift of Tongues.**
ix). **gift of interpreting Different Tongues.**

These different gifts of the Holy Spirit are available to the entire family of God. They are supernatural gifts, which if applied respectively or in combination, will accomplish amazing results in the body of Christ.

They are not just burdens forcibly laid on the shoulders of unwilling believers but constitute spiritual tools and weapons given for service in God's kingdom. These are gifts to be desired and used regularly to the glory of God.

The embers of God's spiritual presence within the child of faith must be kept burning like fire. Their flames must never be allowed to die. They must be constantly stirred, and deliberately too, if they must be useful.

So, believers are encouraged to earnestly desire these abilities, which are special means through which God readily manifests himself to the Church, and to all mankind.

> *"If ye then, being evil, know how to give good gifts unto your children, how much more shall your Father which is in heaven give good things to them that ask him?" (Matthew 7: 11).*

God is a giver. He showed this in his selfless release of his Son as a gift to humanity to save perishing souls. He also promised to send the Holy Spirit and fulfilled this pledge. Some of his blessings are providential in nature and are enjoyed by believers and unbelievers alike.

In addition to these spiritual gifts, the Christian can produce other supernatural fruit by living in harmony with the Holy Spirit. These are supernatural virtues that manifest in lives changed by Christ. They represent the evidence of the overflow of the Holy Spirit in a life that he indwells. So, the believer who has received the gift or gifts of the Holy Ghost must not stifle their manifestations.

No Christian with the gift of God should allow anyone,

believers or unbelievers alike, to bully, intimidate, or limit his effectiveness. Rather, they should boldly step out in faith, declaring God's word as they are empowered by his Spirit.

Oppositions from within the Church, and persecutions from without can pose un-necessary diversions, when a Christian's spiritual gift begins to manifest. But a Holy Spirit gifted believer must persevere, guard his gift, treasure it, be focused, and apply it and leave God to play his own part.

PRAYER POINTS

1). My Father, do not cast me away from your presence, in Jesus name.

2). O Lord, do not take your Holy Spirit away from me, in Jesus name.

3). O Lord, restore the joy of your Salvation to me, in Jesus name.

4). O God that put your Spirit in me, sustain me in every department, in Jesus name.

5). Audible voice of God, speak to my situation, in Jesus name.

6). Flame of fire, consume all my problems, in Jesus name.

7). Pillar of cloud, lead me in my journey by day, in Jesus name.

8). Pillar of fire, lead me as I travel by night, in Jesus name.

9). Finger of God confuse all my detractors, in Jesus name.

10).Shadow of the Almighty God protect my life, in Jesus name.

11). Promise of God manifest in my life, in Jesus name.

12).Holy Spirit, come to my rescue whenever I am in trouble, in Jesus name.

13).Power that delivered Paul and Silas, come and deliver me, in Jesus name.

14).O God that gives good gifts, give me my own, in Jesus name.

SIX

Characteristics of the Holy Spirit.

1). **He is a person.**

The Holy Spirit is a person. This means that he possesses distinguishing personality traits such as will, intellect and emotion. As a result, he engages in all personal and relational activities that define living beings. That is to say, he can think, speak, pray, give gifts, teach, witness, be lied to, grieve, love and even mourn as the situation warrants.

But because he exists in spirit-form, he has no physical body. As a result, he cannot be perceived with natural human eyes. But this does not make him a mystical, ethereal-substance, influence or force as many people think.

He is a divine Being, in the same nature and divine character as Jesus and shares all the qualities that define God the Father. And only a person can do what the Holy Spirit does, like teaching, instructing, command and comfort. Note also that in most scriptures, he is described with personal pronouns.

"Howbeit when he, the Spirit of truth, is come, he will guide you into all truth: for he shall not speak of himself; but whatsoever he shall hear, that shall

*he speak: and he will shew you things to come. He
shall glorify me: for he shall receive of mine, and
shall shew it unto you" (John 16: 13-14).*

When Jesus spoke to his disciples about his replacement by
the Holy Spirit, he promised would send them another comforter.
In that context, Jesus spoke of "another" divine person. The word,
"another" in that promise, points to someone or something of the
same image, nature and likeness just like himself.

So, in introducing the Holy Spirit to his early disciples in
the Bible, Jesus not only spoke of him as a divine-Being of equal
character but repeatedly used the personal pronoun whenever he
talked about him.

*"But when the Comforter is come, whom I will
send unto you from the Father, even the Spirit
of truth, which proceedeth from the Father, he
shall testify of me" (John 15:26).*

The Holy Spirit, from all available scriptures existed in
eternity before the universe was created. He is immortal and is
self-endowed with all the unique attributes of God. Because he
possesses a soul, he expresses emotions of thought, feeling and
knowledge amongst other mental, and spiritual instincts.

*"But the fruit of the Spirit is love, joy, peace,
longsuffering, gentleness, goodness, faith"
(Galatians 5: 22).*

And beyond possessing the virtue of love, the Holy Spirit, like
God the Father and God the Son, is the spirit of love. As a result,
he has the power to produce the fruit of love in those he indwells.

A good tree is known by its fruit. So, one major quality that is typical of the Holy Spirit is the virtue of love.

> *"A good tree cannot bring forth evil fruit, neither can a corrupt tree bring forth good fruit" (Matthew 7: 18).*

2). **He loves.**

The Holy Spirit is a person with tender-loving, passion as God. He is capable of expressing selfless, unconditional, supernatural love, just as the Father and the Son. And he is the means through whom God spreads his deep, invaluable, feeling of affection amongst people of faith.

Through the Holy Spirit, God's authentic love is revealed to Christians, enabling them to experience an affectionate attachment to their creator. This is why believers can enjoy divine grace in a world filled with hate, rejection and bitterness. Indeed, no man can love his neighbor or humanity until his heart is filled with the love of the Holy Spirit.

The Holy Spirit kind of love is not like the carnal feelings by someone of same family or the sentimental connection for another person of different gender. If it was so, there will be no hate or revulsion toward others of different race, age or social class.

But it is a divine expression of compassion that is full of the selfless nature of Christ. It is not love as defined by the flesh, but a cogent, strong, and compelling affection that is more concerned for the needs of others than for oneself. It is love that loves like Jesus did, and only the Holy Spirit can make a person love this way.

This is the kind of love that makes peace, produces longsuffering, inspires gentleness, bears forth goodness, exercises faith, is incubated in meekness and acts with temperance. Through the shedding of this love, the Holy Spirit prepares the souls of men for rebirth in the Son and reconciliation with the Father.

His heart of love is full of mercy as he tenderly reaches out to people of all ethnicities, faith-groups, backgrounds and lifestyles. He even closely embraces people considered as cold-hearted, loveless and the unlovable, with his warm, unconditional grace. This way, he leads souls out of darkness into the marvelous light of God.

> *"Now hope does not disappoint, because the love of God has been poured out in our hearts by the Holy Spirit who was given to us"* *(Romans 5:5).*

The best revelation of divine love is seen in God's selfless gift of his only Son, Jesus Christ, to all humanity. This is the love that God has for all believers. It is the Holy Spirit type of Love, is beyond human imagination and cannot be measured by any scientific yardstick.

The Holy Spirit type of love involves the highest acts of sacrifice, deliberate generosity, humility, empathy, and compassion. It is love which senses human emotions, identifies with their hurtful feelings and responds appropriately to their situation. It does not expect anything in return for any favors, is patient and full of immeasurable kindness. This is the very noble cord that binds the Trinity in unity.

Love is the highest attribute of God's essence and the greatest of all spiritual gifts. The Holy Spirit manner of love is the same godly-affection by which God embraces his children. No wonder Jesus considered the greatest commandment as the love for God, and for one's neighbor.

It is only through the endowment of the Holy Spirit that any Christian can operate by this standard divine affection for himself, others in the church, his neighbor or society. This love is inestimable, invaluable, incomprehensible, limitless, reliable, and counts no costs

Christians demonstrate this divine love by selflessly serving God in humility and living in total obedience to his word. This is one meaningful way any believer can express that likeness of God the Father, which was poured into his life by God the Holy Spirit, when he received God the Son, as Lord and Savior.

It is God's delight to see his children overflow with intimate affection for one another and even for their neighbors. Every Christian can achieve this just by the deliberately showing deep, selfless affection to others of different race, class and even people of other political and religious affiliations.

3). **He thinks**.

The mind is the center of all knowledge. And being in the nature of God, the Holy Spirit has a mind that has privileged knowledge of the Father's will. As a result of this divine ability he comprehends all spiritual truths, natural facts, thoughts and imaginations.

Because of his divine intellect, he has infinite knowledge of all things, a complete understanding of all complexities and insight to perceive things whether in the natural sphere or in the supernatural realm. In this capacity, nothing can be hidden from him. Thus, when he intercedes for a person, he does so from the privileged position of knowing what delights the heart of God and how best to present the individual's matter.

> *"And he that searcheth the hearts knoweth what is the mind of the Spirit, because he maketh intercession for the saints according to the will of God"* (Romans 8: 27).

The holy Spirit played a great role in the creation of man and the universe. He is the divine breath that gave life to all humans, and the indwelling spirit in all believers. As a result, he has un unhindered access into every Christian soul and therefore knows what anyone is thinking or imagining at any particular time.

4). **He reasons.**

The Holy Spirit possesses all distinguishing attributes of personality. This includes a soul that enables him to operate according to his will. He makes decisions and gives instructions according to his will, but cannot be exploited, bewitched or manipulated as is the case with the natural man.

> *"But all these worketh that one and the selfsame Spirit, dividing to every man severally as he will" (1 Corinthians 12:11).*

> *"Now when they had gone throughout Phrygia and the region of Galatia, and were forbidden of the Holy Ghost to preach the word in Asia, After they were come to Mysia, they assayed to go into Bithynia: but the Spirit suffered them not (Acts 16: 6-7).*

The Holy Spirit has a will and is capable of thinking, directing, knowing, and feeling things in the manner that the natural man does. He is the person that decides which child of God receives what spiritual gifts and directs ministerial activities that in ways that benefit the Christian and the body of Christ.

He has a conscience and distinguishes between what is good and that which is evil. He has the divine capacity to make assessments and take decisions for the best benefit of a Christian and the church.

"For it seemed good to the Holy Ghost, and to us, to lay upon you no greater burden than these necessary things" (Acts 15: 28).

This scripture reveals what can happen in a church or to a Christian in times of confusion and how waiting for and following the leading of the Holy Spirit can make a whole lot of difference. It is very helpful that believers trust the leading of the Holy Spirit and not rely on their carnal interpretation of the word of God.

A person can be better at his gift as he puts it to work for the church. But it is the Holy Spirit that decides who gets what gifts, directs how it can be applied and determines what can be accomplished at any time in question, in order to glorify God.

5). **He can grieve.**

The human mind is generally described by practitioners of spiritual warfare as the battle ground of life. Unfortunately, it can easily be high-jacked by the devil in a life that is less concerned with God's righteous standards. This will lead to sin and incur the wrath of God.

The Holy Spirit is a divine person. Every person will be sad or angry to be disappointed by someone he loves. In the same way, the believer who rebels against God will grieve his Spirit. Sadly, many Christians do this all the time by engaging in ungodly acts. By acts of rebellion, believers defile the image of God in them and grieve the Holy Spirit who hates sin.

To grieve means to make a person sad, sorrowful; to cause pain or bring distress. This will happen where there is bitterness of heart, resentfulness, dissentions, un-controlled anger, and irreconcilable differences. Such attitudes make Christians victims of satanic attack, causing the Holy Spirit to be sad.

Worldly corruption, evil thoughts and imaginations, lying, deceits, false witness, put blemishes on souls born of water and by the Holy Ghost. Any of these will tamper with the seal of the Holy Ghost whereby such Christians were sealed unto the day of redemption.

All evil thoughts, words, and actions will negatively affect the heart of God towards the believer. Ignorance of this reality is not an excuse and will lead to actions that offend the righteous standard of the god-head. The Christian who defiles himself by bringing reproach to the name of God will grieve the Holy Spirit, ruin his relationship with God, and bring the consequences of his action upon himself.

> *"And grieve not the holy Spirit of God, whereby ye are sealed unto the day of redemption"* (Ephesians 4: 30).

The Holy Spirit serves as a divine seal. In this manner, he certifies the Christian as belonging to God. He is evidence of the covenant between such a believer and God, serving as the divine signature of approval of such convert's genuine confession of faith.

But the security he provides can be made in-effective when sin comes into play in that believer's life. In such a condition, the Christian becomes vulnerable to the Devil, causing the Holy Spirit to be sad and in distress. By nature, the divine Trinity is holy. So, the Holy Spirit will not condone any impure thoughts, secret sins, or perverse acts due to his hatred for sin. This is because, transgression breaks the heart of God.

So, the Holy Spirit deeply grieves when a Christian engages in willing acts of unrighteousness. Some habits that can make the Holy Spirit sorrowful include keeping malice, engaging in gossip, speaking obscenities, using foul language, listening to all forms of vulgarity, cursing and enjoying abusive behaviors.

"Let no corrupt communication proceed out of your mouth, but that which is good to the use of edifying, that it may minister grace unto the hearers. And grieve not the holy Spirit of God, whereby ye are sealed unto the day of redemption. Let all bitterness, and wrath, and anger, and clamour, and evil speaking, be put away from you, with all malice: And be ye kind one to another, tenderhearted, forgiving one another, even as God for Christ's sake hath forgiven you" (Ephesians 4: 29-32).

"But they rebelled, and vexed his holy Spirit: therefore he was turned to be their enemy, and he fought against them" (Isaiah 63: 10)

Many Christians do not fully understand God's recognition of their bodies as his temple. A person that is God's temple must realize that he is host to the Spirit of God. So, when such a believer transgresses against God's word, he grieves God's Spirit that is inside of him.

"Know ye not that ye are the temple of God, and that the Spirit of God dwelleth in you?" (1 Corinthians 3: 16).

The Christian, his local church assembly, and entire faith community are described in the word of God as temples. As hosts of the Holy Spirit therefore, they should not accommodate evil of any type or measure. Any such transgression will defile God's temple and grieve the Holy Spirit.

If a person, Church, or nation is defiled by sin, the gifts of God will cease to flow there. It may not happen swiftly, but soon the inevitable silence of the Holy Spirit will become glaring in that place of worship. The result is that the person, prophets in that church or nation cease to hear from God. Prophecies become fake, dishonest testimonies abound, divisions among members appear, and crippling controversies arise within the body of Christ.

Since the Holy Spirit is an eternal gift to believers of the New Testament, he does not depart from a Christian on condition of offences. But sin will cause him to grieve and limit him from accomplishing anything in that rebellious soul. The devil will take advantage of any situation where the free flow of the Holy Spirit is caged. For this reason, Christians are forewarned of the consequences of such evil.

God is the only source of absolute righteousness. And given this reality, any form of sin translates into affront against the god-head. So, when a Christian rejects God's word, he offends the Holy Spirit which dwells inside of him. This will no doubt lead to the suspension of divine privileges, promises, benefits, and loss of the genuine experience of God's love, peace, power and joy of the Holy Ghost.

6). **The Holy Spirit can be quenched**.

Willful transgression against God's commandment will limit the activity of the Holy Spirit. In this mournful mood, he is restricted from doing what he is wired to do. This will unleash problems as acts that desecrate sacred principles and violate divine laws have potentials to unlock God's wrath.

Sin has as much power to quench the holy-fire in any believer's life, in the same manner that righteous-living can ignite goodness. So, the Holy Spirit mourns when a believer commits sin, grieving for that soul which the devil desires to destroy.

Grieving the Holy Spirit frustrates holy power, weakens divine authority and undermines the divine character of obedience. It erodes the very fundamental pillars of trust upon which the Christian intimacy with God is founded.

Enemies of God's law will relish at the opportunity to cause his Spirit to mourn. Those who disdain divine authority will be delighted to see God. And every human admiration for disobedience, which is the primary weapon used by Satan to destroy God's children, will bring sorrow to the heart of the Holy Spirit.

Human habits of bitterness, rage, anger, harsh words, malice towards one another, and divisions in the Church will grieve the Holy Spirit. These vices defile our bodies which God describes as his temple, in which also his Spirit resides.

So, in order not to quench the operation of the Holy Spirit, Christians are persuaded to express the virtuous characters of love, kindness, compassion. And they must obey the command to forgive one another, even as Christ forgave sinners.

7). **The Holy Spirit can be resisted.**

The Holy Spirit is happy when he is recognized in fellowship. But he feels rejected when he is resisted or neglected. He desires and deserves every believer's friendship and fellowship. This is what brings strength in times of spiritual weakness and courage to overcome low-moral. That is why he should not be resisted.

> *"ye stiffnecked and uncircumcised in heart and ears, ye do always resist the holy ghost: as your fathers did, so do ye" (Acts 7: 51).*

The desire to know the Holy Spirit will meet with academic obstacles, scientific road-blocks and even religious-denominational resentments. But this should not be considered as uncommon because it existed even in ancient cultures which sought, through the tenets of their belief systems, to create false equivalences between the duality of their deities and the concept of divine trinity.

Unfortunately, neither the limited understanding of the human mind, science-based evaluations of psychology, nor the geometric theories of astrology have come close to comprehending the mystery behind the existence of this one God who exists in three dimensions.

Those who resist, reject, despise, neglect, or outrightly denounce the existence of the Holy Spirit, deny themselves of countless blessings and privileges he bestows. That is why churches in that league never experience the fire of his fellowship, charm of his love, joy of his presence, passion of his grace, the awe of his person or encounter the feeling of his raw power.

Only the souls that connect with God through the person of The Holy Spirit gain the unmerited understanding of his divine mysteries. These are the ones to whom the secrets of God are revealed through his Spirit. They are the people he guides, whose thoughts he directs and who he teaches the art of profitable prayer. And their worship is blessed with spiritual life.

Knowing the Holy Spirit helps a person to understand the secrets of God's kingdom. That is why that knowledge is a privilege reserved mainly for people of faith. Only God can reveal himself to those he desires through the works of the Holy Spirit.

The flame of the Holy Spirit revives the believer's soul by setting his faith ablaze for Christ. He is the divine instrument that endues Christians with power for ministry and baptizes them with fire to do exploits. His gifts reveal the power and presence of the divine Trinity. Without him, worship is empty, the Christian is weak, and the church dies from spiritual malnutrition.

8). **The Holy Spirit can be lied to.**

The Holy Spirit is a person and shows emotions. And it can grieve his heart when believers lie, assuming that he will not find out. He knows what is in the heart of all men, so no one can get away with a lie to him. The sad story of Ananias and his wife, Sapphira, is a good illustration of attempts by believers to lie to the Holy Spirit. It also shows what the consequences can be.

> *"But Peter said, Ananias, why hath Satan filled thine heart to lie to the Holy Ghost, and to keep back part of the price of the land? Whiles it remained, was it not thine own? and after it was sold, was it not in thine own power? why hast thou conceived this thing in thine heart? thou hast not lied unto men, but unto God"* (Acts 5:3-4)

9). **He has knowledge.**

Every human soul is credited with ability to will, feel, think, and to know. But considering that knowledge is the exclusive preserve of God, no person other than members of the divine Trinity can understand the mind of God. this only comes by revelation.

The Holy Spirit, in his Omni-scent nature, possesses this ability inherent only in the divine nature, to reveal hidden knowledge. This virtue enables him to know, understand, and reveal secrets that God desires to show his children in ways no celestial being, angel or human soul can do.

While these traits of perception may seem naturally common, the demonstration of them by the Holy Spirit exceeds that of the natural mind, whose capacity to know, hear, feel, say, and understand things is un-limited.

> *"But as it is written, Eye hath not seen, nor ear heard, neither have entered into the heart of man, the things which God hath prepared for them that love him. But God hath revealed them unto us by his Spirit: for the Spirit searcheth all things, yea, the deep things of God. For what man knoweth the things of a man, save the spirit of a man which is in him? even so the things of God knoweth no man, but the Spirit of God (1Corinthians 2: 9-11)".*

No matter how knowledgeable, intelligent or wise the human mind is, it is limited by nature in perceiving spiritual things, even when such things are to his advantage. Only the Holy Spirit can reveal the things of God to those whom he desires to show such things. The Holy Spirit is the person with such divine ability to play this role.

He is the spiritual binoculars through whom humanity can peep into the sacred heart of God. It is through him that any meaningful vision or revelation can be received, and knowledge and divine wisdom be possessed.

Truly, knowledge of the nature, character, and person of God is beyond human understanding. But through the help of the Holy Spirit, the mind of the eternal, Sovereign and self-existing God is made known to those he chooses.

As a member of the Trinity, the Holy Spirit is of God, works with God, and is the channel through whom God the Father discloses his thoughts, and expresses divine presence to humanity.

10). **He is God's excellent spirit.**

No person can properly instruct another individual on matters of the divine family, except that person rightly knows, deeply understands and adequately appreciates the mind of God. But the Holy Spirit is dully qualified in these aspects and passes them on to God's children.

In him is the excellent spirit to instruct God's children and the unlimited knowledge to teach them all truth. This was the key to prophet Daniel's splendid accomplishments. This dominant factor in Daniel's character explains why he was highly favored in the land of Babylon, even though he was a slave. The spirit to excel above all others derives from God. Daniel was a slave, yet he operated greatly in this gift. This is the unmerited gift the Holy Spirit gives to the redeemed believer.

11). **The Holy Spirit speaks.**

The Holy Spirit is the Spirit of God. So, he knows the mind of the Father. He is the voice through whom God speaks to humanity. Through his gift of prophesy, mere men can hear what God desires in his mind and declare it to the church in particular. Often times, this can be beneficial to all mankind.

The Holy Spirit speaks. He may not sound loud all the time, but he is clear when he speaks, and his voice is convicting of human need for Christ. For what he says is the will of God by which he leads, teaches, guides, and directs people in the paths of righteousness.

Through his word, believers receive wise counsel, knowledge and understanding in spiritual things. This helps them overcome temptation and motivates believers to a life of godliness. He can speak through certain life's events, in dreams, by visions, or revelations.

"Then the Spirit said unto Philip, Go near, and join thyself to this chariot" (Acts 8: 29).

The Holy Spirit is Christ's witness who passes on what he hears from heaven to the inner-man of a child of God. Christians led by what they hear from the Holy Spirit are very successful in every area of life. They live in the peace of God which excludes worry and anxiety.

12). **The holy Spirit is a humble Being.**

Biblical descriptions of the activities of the Holy Spirit show that he commands unlimited spiritual power. Despite this unique character, he is very gentle, humble, works inconspicuously and is content with playing divine, background roles.

He does not speak of himself but is greatly involved in the revelation of God and assisting believers understand the works of Jesus. Through these relentless functions, he inspires believers for a committed life of fruit-bearing for Christ.

By glorifying the Lord Jesus rather than himself, the Holy Spirit teaches Christians the humility of Christ, enables them to do the will of the Father, and helps them in their honest moves of surrendering evil works and desires to God.

Furthermore, the Holy Spirit assists believers in their desire to follow in Christ's footsteps of unfeigned love, selfless-sacrifice and obedient service. Any believer indwelled by the Holy Spirit will walk on his Christian journey without struggles.

13). **He is the Anointing.**

An anointed person is someone set apart for specific purpose or task. Such persons in the Old Testament included Kings, Prophets, Priests, and children of Israel. But in this New Testament dispensation, all Christians, by their heritage in Christ and the indwelling of the Holy Spirit are carriers of God's anointing.

God is the anointer, the one who's authority is invested on a chosen individual, tabernacle, vestments or sacred furniture of worship. The Holy Spirit is the anointing and Jesus Christ is the Messiah, the anointed one of God.

While the anointing of God upon a person confers such divine privileges as protection, provision and direction to name a few special rights, it is not an insurance against fallibility, neither is it guarantee against satanic challenges.

Samson the Nazarite who judged Israel for about Twenty years, is a good illustration. Though he was called from the womb and anointed to lead God's chosen people, he came to self-destruction, driven by the lust of his eyes.

But Jesus excelled when he was anointed by the same Spirit of God. The Bible says he went about preaching the good news of salvation, healing the sick, opening blind eyes, and delivering those bound by the devil.

"How God anointed Jesus of Nazareth with the Holy Ghost and with power: who went about doing good, and healing all that were oppressed of the devil; for God was with him" *(Acts 10: 38).*

The powerful gospel message preached by the Apostle Peter to the Gentile congregation in Cornelius' house, testified of the greatness of the anointing that God bestowed upon Jesus of Nazareth. That anointing did not dry up at the cross or return to heaven at Christ's ascension. He is still available to all believers. He is the Holy Spirit.

PRAYER POINTS

1). As the Lord lives, I shall not grieve the Holy Spirit, in Jesus name.

2). Holy Spirit of the living God, help me to guard my heart with diligence, in Jesus name.

3). Holy Spirit, teach me to speak with wisdom, in Jesus name.

4). Holy Spirit, sharpen my mind to reason properly, in Jesus name.

5). O God, order my steps to work in the right places, in Jesus name.

6). As the Lord lives, I Shall not sit in the seat of the scornful, in Jesus name.

7). As the Lord lives, I shall not walk in the counsel of the wicked, in Jesus name.

8). Holy Spirit, give me speed to flee from every appearance of evil, in Jesus name.

9). O Lord, give me power to overcome in times of temptation, in Jesus name.

10). Holy Spirit help me to always surrender my will to God's will, in Jesus name.

11). As the Lord lives, I shall not quench the operations of the Holy Spirit in my life, in Jesus name.

12). I resist anything prompting me to resist the move of the Holy Spirit, in Jesus name.

13). The Devil shall not take the seat of the Holy Spirit in my life, in Jesus name.

14). O God, reveal mysteries to me through the Holy Spirit, in Jesus name.

CHAPTER

SEVEN

Works of the Holy Spirit

Beyond available Bible records, there are numerous human testimonies of positive, spiritual transformations accomplished in the faith community, by the Holy Spirit, to the glory of God. The methods he employed in bringing these feats to pass are generally referred to as the "Works of the Holy Spirit". The "works" here, describe what the Holy Spirit does and how he does them.

These works will be explained in this chapter. But it is important to clear the false impression, at this point that the Holy Spirit works only for Christians and through them. No. he can work through any person or vessel of his choice. This is because even the initial work of salvation in a reprobate soul, is by the intervention of the Holy Spirit.

So, whether a person is a Christian or not, the Spirit of God can work with and through anyone to fulfill divine purpose. He worked in King Ahasuerus, causing him to remember Mordecai, in King Cyrus who expedited and funded the return of the Jews, to rebuild the city of Jerusalem. There are other evidences of his works found in the Old and the New Testaments.

In ancient Egypt, for instance, the Holy Spirit of God worked on the Pharaoh that ruled that Empire during the slavery and incarceration of Joseph. He was also the vessel that prepared the heart of a Pharaoh's daughter, to rescue and adopt Moses. Neither of these Pharaohs believed in the God of Abraham, Isaac and Jacob.

During the reign of Nebuchadnezzar, King of Babylon, four Hebrew slaves Daniel, Misael, Azariah, and Hananiah were lifted from positions of bondage and made advisers in the royal palace. This was because, the Holy Spirit used his gift in these boys to correctly discern and interpret the king's dream, which feat was beyond the Kings magicians and astrologers.

> *"Then the king Nebuchadnezzar fell upon his face, and worshipped Daniel, and commanded that they should offer an oblation and sweet odours unto him. The king answered unto Daniel, and said, Of a truth it is, that your God is a God of gods, and a Lord of kings, and a revealer of secrets, seeing thou couldest reveal this secret" (Daniel 2: 46- 47).*

Following this accomplishment, King Nebuchadnezzar promoted Daniel and his three Hebrew "brothers". He also honored Daniel's God, for Daniel had given credit to the Sovereign God for this uncommon feat which they achieved by the power of his Holy Spirit.

In some cases, the Holy Spirit used the privileged positions of some ungodly persons to favor or discipline God's chosen people. And in other circumstances, he operated through leaders of gentile nations to protect his divine interest in the lives of God's people.

God often works in many mysterious ways to reveal himself to his people. But in all of them, he does so through the person of the Holy Spirit. There are numerous ways through which the Holy Spirit operates, but only a few will be considered here.

1). **He guides people to the new birth in Christ.**

The Holy Spirit is always fully involved in every matter that connects humanity to God. He is the bridge that links the natural man to the supernatural presence of God and the instrument that God uses to initiate the process of the new birth in Christ.

He is the Spirit that bears witness of Jesus. And because he speaks directly to human hearts concerning Christ, he makes converts and prepares them to become sound witnesses of the truth which proceeds from God.

Through him, the door to an unbeliever's heart is opened to welcome Christ and the gift of salvation. In times past, he opened doors of opportunities for apostles and evangelists enabling them to take the Gospel all over the world that then existed.

No one can be born again without the prompting of a "believing faith" by the Holy Spirit. This believing faith is a gift from God which every person is endowed with at birth. It is this spiritual factor which the Holy Spirit ignites at the ripe time, enabling a positive response to God's invitation to experience the new-birth experience.

Believing faith is a divine gift deposited in all persons at the instant of parental conception. However, it is the stirring of this "inherent gift" in due time, either by the Holy Spirit, another person of faith, or some circumstance of life that the irresistible urge to receive Christ is awakened.

Through the intermediary of the Holy Spirit, any unregenerate soul can be convicted and convinced of the need for spiritual rebirth. So, beyond the natural birth which is physical, the souls of every descendant from the fallen Adam and Eve, need spiritual re-birth in Christ before reconciliation with God can take place.

Spiritual birth in Christ is a gift of God through the help of the Holy Spirit. But it is by the stirring of the gift of "believing faith" that human souls become reachable for God.

The Holy Spirit makes it easy for every soul in our human society to be within reach of the gospel message. This outreach has been made much easier with the advent of social media, greatly supported by the internet, television and telephones

2). **The Holy Spirit prepares believers for kingdom service.**

The Holy Spirit empowers Christians for service in the kingdom of God. Only once in biblical record were people baptized with the power of the Holy Spirit before they received the new-birth experience.

Even then, those upon whom this power came, were uncertain with what to do with the unprecedented manifestations they experienced. So, Cornelius and his house-hold members were not alone in their timidity. The early church disciples were also amazed in their very first encounter with this baptism of power.

Jesus promised his disciples they would experience an outburst of power after the baptism with the Holy Ghost. This spiritual event was the fulfilment of that promise. And as the first of its kind in history, no one knew what to expect. Even the witnesses who stood around did not understand the expression of the disciples and thought they were drunk.

Jesus' early disciples were just ordinary people. They were not among the elite group in their society considered as religious by any standard. But when the Holy Spirit came upon them, he baptized these very common people with such uncommon power they began to accomplish uncommon feat.

Through the works of the Holy Spirit, he confers recipients with unique power to perform spiritual assignments that amaze beyond expectations. With this power, disciples accomplish remarkable exploits and make astonishing sacrifice beyond natural abilities.

The transforming power of the Holy Spirit opens the door of trust required for a deep intimacy with God. It confers boldness to work for him, confidence to run with the message of the gospel without looking back and strength that cannot be wearied.

He prepares a believer for the working of signs, miracles, and wonders in un-expected places and at uncertain times. And when this power incubates the natural man, it fills him with supernatural abilities that make him perform deeds beyond human limits.

In 1993, I was in a church one Sunday morning in Houston, Texas. And just as the service was rounding up, a sister passed out. It was an embarrassing moment seeing other worshippers running away from her, instead of gathering to pray with her. Even the lady's husband was confused and did not know what to do.

For some reason, the pastor of that church never liked me. And even though he was the senior pastor while I was an ordinary member who sometimes led in prayer sessions, he struggled with the way the congregation responded when I prayed, compared to when he did. But I refused to be troubled by his observations and comparisons.

As a Pentecostal congregation that believes in deliverance ministration, I expected the pastor to take the lead, while others helped, but he scurried into his office and asked one of the ushers to get me. His instruction was, "tell that man to go and prove himself".

Unfortunately for him, I was already on my knees praying for the sister before the message came. I got two others praying with me and in a about ten minutes, which looked though like a whole day, the sister's eyes rolled in their socket and her stiff and almost cold body came back to life. I did not have to prove myself because I knew the Holy Spirit will not embarrass the church.

He prepares willing believers ahead of situations like the one I just described. And his astonishing power is what transforms the ordinary natural man into an extra-ordinary person with capacity to break new barriers, cut through spiritual boarders and make what things that were thought to be impossibilities, to become realities.

3). **The Holy Spirit testifies of Christ.**

The scriptures confirm that Jesus Christ physically left the earth and ascended into heaven after his ministry, death, and resurrection. Prior to his leaving however, he promised to send the Holy Spirit to take his place.

His disciples were instructed to wait in the city of Jerusalem until the fulfilment of "the promise of the Father", which Jesus said would endow all current and future believers with necessary power to effectively serve in God's kingdom.

So, on that first Pentecost after Christ's ascension, while his disciples were gathered in the upper-room in anticipation of this promise, a sound "like a mighty rushing wind" with cloven tongues that looked life fire, suddenly came from heaven and sat on each of them.

That day, every disciple present was filled with the Holy Ghost. And as a sign, they all spoke with other tongues as the Spirit of God gave them utterance. This crucial public event was generally corroborated by a gathering of witnesses who heard the illiterate disciples speaking in languages alien to them.

By sending the Holy Spirit whom Christ described as "another Comforter" (as his worthy replacement), Jesus ensured that no spiritual void was left on earth after his departure to his Father.

The Holy Spirit has since continued to sustain Christ's earthly ministry with the cooperation of disciples from one generation of proselytes to another generation of converts. Testifying about Jesus is a major work of the Holy Spirit. And he will continue to play this role until Christ returns again for his church.

4). **He is the spirit of truth.**

It is undeniable that truth has become a scarce commodity in this electronic age. In these modern times, human society is hastily heading down the spiral trail of self-destruction because what is true no longer has value in spiritual and political communities.

The truth has practically been banished in our once revered spiritual institutions, in court-rooms, public gatherings, the media, and places that were once considered as honorable.

In our world, people no longer appreciate the concept of objective truth. Children now live by the lies they heard their parents tell severally and double down on the lies regardless of opportunities to redeem their integrity.

The tragedy of the already ugly situation is that even those at the highest level of authority, including people who claim to be Christians, now use the new but dangerous and immoral vocabulary called "alternative facts".

The truth-crises that humanity is facing right in this generation has reached the height of global calamity. Unfortunately, the church, which is not exempted from this heinous dilemma with its massive spiritual implications, has continued to act with a disgraceful attitude of indifference.

But thank God for the Holy Spirit; that Spirit of Truth which proceeds from God who cannot lie. Through the Holy Spirit, every child of God can absolutely find consolation in such dark days as the world now lives in.

Because all truth procced from God through the Holy Spirit, he can explain the truth of the word of God in a manner that makes it understandable, simple, clear and easily applicable.

He is responsible for interpreting God's inerrant word to the church and he does so in ways that reveal its irrefutable reality. And he applies God's truth to illuminate the divine paths for Christians. This saves Christians from embracing false doctrines that lead souls away from godliness.

He teaches God's truth with undoubtable evidence and clarity that those who hear his testimony of Christ, quickly believe him in their hearts. This makes such people to gladly confess him with their mouth, readily accepting God's gift of salvation without doubt.

In a generation obsessed with worldliness and lost on the fast lane of carnal immorality, most "kindergarten Christians" scarcely have useful time to spiritually renew their souls with God's word. As such, it is very easy to find believers who even in adulthood, have no deep relationship with God.

This starts with dwindling fellowship with the God of the word, gradually progressing to mindlessness to his commandments, until such individuals get to where human rules take pre-eminence over divine law, spiritual statutes, and moral principles.

> *"Now the Spirit speaketh expressly, that in the latter times some shall depart from the faith, giving heed to seducing spirits, and doctrines of devils: (1 Timothy 4:1).*

True to the teachings of the Apostle Paul, a lot has changed for the worse since his letter to Apostle Timothy. Currently, much evil doctrine has infiltrated the church. It is even widely taught, and openly tolerated just as the apostle cautioned.

In the early years of the church formation, false teachers were a menace against truth and godliness. In these modern times, they have increased in number, grown in authority, and are engaging more seriously in the business of misleading people with lying wonders while wreaking great damage to the body of Christ.

In treacherous times like these, it is the Holy Spirit that steps in to separate facts from the truth and to reveal in plain terms, what is true as against what is false. He is the divine instrument for affirming God's word and for declaring it in a vivid manner that eliminates doubt.

In the Old Testament era, the Holy Spirit was God's evidence to his children through the prophets. But in this dispensation, he speaks clearly through regenerated souls who have now become sons and daughters of God.

5). He reveals the mind of God.

The Holy Spirit is the channel through which the mind of God is revealed to the natural man. The word of God comes from the spirit of God. That explains why sin-stained, reprobate souls or ordinary intellectual minds cannot understand the things of God.

> *"But as it is written, Eye hath not seen, nor ear heard, neither have entered into the heart of man, the things which God hath prepared for them that love him. but God hath revealed them unto us by the Spirit: for the Spirit searcheth all things, yea, the deep things of God" (1 Corinthians 2: 9).*

The absence of the Holy Spirit hinders the discernment of spiritual things. When this is the case, a wide gap is created, separating a child of faith from the presence of God. This is when the word of God begins to appear foolish to the carnal man.

But when the Holy Spirit is in place in a life, he empowers that believer to get regular peeps into the mind of God, giving him privileged knowledge of supernatural activities such as thoughts, plans, and intentions.

> *"For who hath known the mind of the Lord, that he may instruct him? but we have the mind of Christ" (1 Corinthians 2: 15).*

The Holy Spirit is the person through whom divine prophecies are released, dreams disclosed, and visions revealed. He is the source behind all manifestation gifts, as well as power for charismatic operations.

6). **The Holy Spirit unifies the church.**

A united church delights the heart of God and brings eternal joy to his kingdom. Church unity is a work of grace and mercy of God, and the Holy Spirit is the person that causes it to come into place. He is the power that unites the church. Just as unity exists in the divine Trinity, he is the binding force in the body of Christ who ensures that Christians cooperate as one. This unity is essential, and its evidence is the reign of divine love, peace, justice, and righteousness.

But the devil will easily prevail against the body of Christ if he can keep it as fragmented as he has achieved so far. This is because he has discovered that there are more things that divide a Christian family riddled with worldliness than keep her together.

So, his focus is on encouraging denominations and fellowships based on racial affiliations, political orientations, sects with same-sexual interests, same attitude to immorality or linked up by same views on parenting, divorce and marriages.

So far, he has succeeded at ensuring that Roman Catholics are not aligned with Anglicans, Lutherans do not collaborate Baptists, the Jehovah Witnesses cannot share pulpit with the Evangelicals, especially due doctrinal differences. To make matters worse, those of the Apostolic faith never agree with the Mormons whom they do not even regard as Christians.

The tenets of Mormonism as laid down by their original founder deviate from the scriptures in not accepting the three persons of the Trinity as same and equal in substance and being. They claim that God the Father was once a mortal man with flesh and bone but progressed to the godhead and became immortal (Numbers 23: 19; Hosea 11: 9; John 4; 24).

Without unity of doctrine, the church will be in complete disarray. And given the current moral condition of this world, the under-current of institutional racism, gender in-equality, and oddities peculiar to religious minded individuals and nations, the devil will have a field day scattering what Christ gathered.

But by putting aside useless doctrinal contentions and selfish human attitudes, the Holy Spirit restrains the church-family from fighting over un-necessary carnal issues that erode unity of brethren. So, what is needed to shut the doors against the enemy of the church is consensus on sacred doctrines, mutual submission in love and respect for one another.

Through the inspired word of God, he reproves believers in kindness, corrects them in love, and properly instructs children of faith in righteousness, ensuring that believers are well established on the foundations of true biblical opinions that help in discerning between good and evil.

He creates that harmonious atmosphere that assists Christians in building mutual trust and concord in the church, enabling the undistracted worship of God in awe and righteousness. These sacred practices attract divine blessings that lead to church growth.

Through the indwelling presence of the Holy Spirit, he sensitizes Christians to develop a mind-set that allows peace to reign within the church-family. And his impact on converts is a meaningful gauge of his presence and realistic tool for measuring the health condition of the body of Christ.

The church is one body called into one faith by one Spirit, to serve one God. She is called to one hope and one baptism through Christ and reconciled to one Father who is over all and in all. This original oneness calls for a bonding that will not crack or be divided.

Through him, the church stands fast in one spirit, striving with one mind, and working together in faith for the smooth spreading of the gospel. It is this one accord in Christ's love, expressed by the Holy Spirit that binds all Christians as one in the kingdom of God.

This is how the Spirit prepares the bride for his coming bridegroom. He patiently equips believers with righteous virtues that make them desire to live in holiness. So, when Jesus eventually returns, he will find a chaste bride that is undefiled, without blemish, wrinkle or spot that is ready and waiting for him.

7). **He is a teacher.**

The Holy Spirit is the believer's teacher. Children of God who learn from him are richly rewarded with spiritual knowledge. This helps believers to navigate the dark places of this world without falling into evil snares. He instructs believers in a manner that makes them equipped and ready for kingdom service.

No Christian can successfully make a convert without being properly coached by the Holy Spirit. Many may not have the pristine language or sound intellectual education to win over lawyers, doctors and engineers. But a Christian that relies on the Holy Spirit will readily be reminded of everything the word of God says about Jesus. "For the Holy Ghost shall teach you in the same hour what ye ought to say" (Luke 12: 12).

> *"But the anointing which ye have received of him abideth in you, and ye need not that any man teach you: but as the same anointing teacheth you of all things, and is truth, and is no lie, and even as it hath taught you, ye shall abide in him" (1 John 2: 27).*

He regularly calls the word of God to remembrance in the hearts of believers, offering better solutions to life's challenges and helping Christians who constantly feed and meditate on it to remain in right-standing with their creator. The Holy Spirit teaches the believers to model their lives based on Christ's word, rather than relying on the blue-print of the world.

Because he knows and understands the deep thoughts of God, he teaches those secret things to believers that God wants to reveal to them. By applying such privileged knowledge, Christians are expected to lead, direct, and guide the body of Christ away from the destructive ways of the world system.

> *"But as it is written, Eye hath not seen, nor ear heard, neither have entered into the heart of man, the things which God hath prepared for them that love him. But God hath revealed them unto us by his Spirit: for the Spirit searcheth all things, yea, the deep things of God. For what man knoweth the things of a man, save the spirit of man which is in him?*

even so the things of God knoweth no man, but the Spirit of God. Now we have received, not the spirit of the world, but the spirit which is of God; that we might know the things that are freely given to us of God. Which things also we speak, not in the words which man's wisdom teacheth, but which the Holy Ghost teacheth; comparing spiritual things with spiritual" *(1Corinthians 2: 10-13).*

8). **He is an intercessor.**

Any form of fatigue or laziness will cause tragic problems in spiritual warfare. That is why the Christian needs the inevitable help of the Holy Spirit. He is a tireless prayer warrior who groans ceaselessly and tirelessly in prayer for believers and for the church, in the presence of God.

He is the spiritual representative whose incessant pleas before the throne of grace procures the vital access ensuring that person who asks, seeks, or knocks, receives attention from God. The voice of the Holy Spirit is what is heard in heaven when a Spirit-filled Christian prays.

"For through him we both have access by one Spirit unto the Father" *(Ephesians 2: 18).*

"And because ye are sons, God hath sent forth the Spirit of his Son into your hearts, crying, Abba, Father" *(Galatians 4:6).*

Quite often, Christians cannot find appropriate words to make their requests or present their matter before God when in difficulty. It is in such situations that the help of the Holy

Spirit becomes inevitable. He is the believer's spiritual mentor, representative and superior prayer partner.

Because he knows the mind of God, he has divine privilege of using the right words that effectively address any situation in question. This way, he presents the believer's needs in the proper manner to attract divine attention and favor.

The Holy Spirit is unquestionably the prime intercessor for the saints. He regularly weeps before the presence of God on behalf of people of faith, employing deep sounds of pain which cannot be uttered.

Part of the reason the Holy Spirit indwells Christians is to provide them with important spiritual assets that most believers lack or do not consider vital as they begin to pray. This is why he is indispensable.

So, while most Christians lack relevant spiritual resources at the altar of prayer, it is the Holy Spirit that comes to the rescue. In such times, He helps believers align their desires with the will of God, rather than allowing them to roam aimlessly at the throne of grace.

"Likewise the Spirit also helpeth our infirmities: for we know not what we should pray for as we ought: but the Spirit itself maketh intercession for us with groanings which cannot be uttered. And he that searcheth the hearts knoweth what is the mind of the Spirit, because he maketh intercession for the saints according to the will of God" (Romans 8 26-27).

To help is to assist, support, guide, advice, and aid a Christian with a view to ensuring that his endeavor is fruitful, pleasant, refreshing, satisfying and cordial. His intervention lends a helping-hand and boosts human efforts, eliminating handicaps and obstructions that stand in the way of prayer.

The Holy Spirit backs-up a person's effort by making his communication with God clearer. He helps bring succor and encouragement to believer who is already praying, giving him hope that his expectation shall be fulfilled. And it can be very gratifying for a Christian to realize that he is regularly supported at the altar of prayer by the Holy Spirit.

While the Holy Spirit employs his supernatural abilities to help children of faith communicate with God, the devil on the other hand will use every tool at his disposal to distract, undermine or completely hinder any kind of fellowship or relationship with the divine deity.

That is why the Christian needs ceaseless spiritual help. This is not a call for spiritual laziness but to reaffirm the need for mutual cooperation between a prayer warrior and the Holy Spirit. He is always ready to assist the believer who kick-starts his prayer.

Without the help of the Holy Spirit, believers will not experience rewarding fellowship with God. Communication at the altar of prayer will be difficult, a struggle, improperly handled, and even providential blessings will seem far to reach.

And when such occurrences become regular, they introduce weakness on the altar of prayer, consequently leading to doubt and mistrust. These are the things that defraud children of faith of victories that Christ already won for the Church on the cross.

The Holy Spirit is therefore the believer's indispensable and most trusted ally in prayer. And any downplaying of his contribution in communication with God will have its immediate as well as long-term, bitter consequences.

9). **He is the Spirit of adoption**

The status of any person changes immediately he experience's the new birth. Following the moment of regeneration, there is an immediate indwelling of the Spirit of God. By this act, heaven testifies that parent-hood has changed hands, as such a person now becomes God's adopted child.

In line with the Christian doctrine of reconciliation, God the Father, by the humble submission of God the Son (Jesus Christ), executed a perfect rescue plan for humanity. But it is through the final seal of the Holy Spirit, that those saved by Christ, are adopted into the family of God.

Adoption is a statutory process whereby a person taken from one family, is accepted into another better estate. In this new family the adopted person is expected to be raised under more comfortable conditions, complete better opportunities unquestionable advantages, privileges, immunities and rights. In the appropriate words of the Apostle Paul:

> *"For you did not receive a spirit that makes you a slave again to fear, but you received the Spirit of adoption. And by him, we cry Abba. Father". (Romans 8: 5).*

Adoption is a compassionate act that makes a helpless soul that was once bound by sin and the Devil to become free in Christ. It is akin to being delivered from poor, careless, oppressive, indifferent and abusive parents, by a kind, loving, wealthy, and compassionate family.

It is a process usually executed by the richer, stronger and a better-placed person in heritage. An adopted person immediately becomes a member of the new family with all the privileges of the latter. This is what the Holy Spirit accomplishes in the life of a person who has accepted Christ.

The moment a new believer gets adopted into the family of God, he loses all former liabilities of his previous family. By his adoption, he becomes a legitimate child of God. By this process, he instantly becomes a joint heir with Christ, conferred with all the rights, privileges, and responsibilities of the family of God.

Jesus sacrificial death on the cross qualified all future believers for adoption by the Holy Spirit. But the process of adoption cannot be accomplished if the Holy Spirit does not play this divine role. It is after he brings a once reprobate person into the family of God through Christ, that such a soul can begin to enjoy his liberties in the kingdom of God.

The concept of adoption illustrates God's amazing acts of mercy, and grace. Divine mercy usually precedes God's grace. Through the way of mercy, he forgives human transgressions and gives believers unlimited access to his presence.

Adoption in the secular world compares to the pattern that exists in the family of God. but while the process in the world can be reversed, annulled or revoked, the pattern in the family of God is irreversible. It involves the permanent conferment of rights, responsibilities and a new identity to the convert, who by reason of salvation is now accepted into the family of God and becomes a co-heir of the promise with God the Son.

> *"For it became him, for whom are all things, and by whom are all things, in bringing many sons unto glory, to make the captain of their salvation perfect through sufferings"* *(Hebrews 2: 10).*

The Holy Spirit is the primary link between a new convert and God. He plays a candid role in God's redemptive plan to assemble sons and daughters of different races, gender, class and tongues, into God's kingdom. And he is the person who initiates, establishes and concludes every process of adoption.

By this process the Holy Spirit causes those who sincerely surrender to Christ to find help in their daily prayer-life and to really experience the joy of salvation. This way, the faith of such converts is strengthened, and their hope sustained as they continue to engage in spiritual life that delight the heart of God.

> *"But ye are not in the flesh, but in the Spirit, if so be that the Spirit of God dwell in you. Now if any man have not the Spirit of Christ, he is none of his" (Romans 8: 9).*

10). He produces fruit in believers.

Nothing positive can happen in to a believer's character without the full cooperation of that soul. But the influence of the Holy Spirit makes all the difference. As he touches souls, he convicts them for Christ, before transforming such lives in a ways no other influence can achieved. And through these changed lives, he impacts the world for Christ.

He is the spiritual beacon that guides people of all races, tongues, and nations to embrace virtuous values, leads them in the fear of God, helps them obey his word, abide in his ways and ensures that they bear fruit worthy of Christ's righteous nature.

To the broken, surrendered, humble, obedient and teachable children of faith, he lavishes necessary spiritual gifts required to witness for Christ and testify of the good news of the kingdom of God. He strengthens these disciples "to run and not be wearied, to walk and not faint".

The person who receives Christ as his Lord and Savior must aspire to be like Jesus in bearing fruit for the Father's kingdom. It is the Holy Spirit that acts as a drill or planter, sowing Christ in men's lives.

He is the sower of good seed in people's hearts and in the end helps to harvest good fruit for Christ. He gives every seed the chance to bear fruit but will prune every branch that consistently fails to bear fruit.

So, it is by the infilling and outpouring of the Holy Spirit that a Christian can produce Christ-like fruit such as love, joy, peace, faithfulness, patience, gentleness, goodness, kindness, and self-control.

PRAYER POINTS.

1). Great Intercessor, pray for me always, in Jesus name.

2). Holy Spirit of God, use me to lead others to Christ, in Jesus name.

3). Seducing spirits following me about be exposed and disgraced, in Jesus name.

4). Monitoring spirits looking for me, become blind and confused, in Jesus name.

5). Holy Spirit of God, anoint me for great works, in Jesus name.

6). Powers distracting me at the altar of prayer receive double destruction, in Jesus name.

7). Powers assigned to take my attention from God, be roasted by Holy Ghost fire, in Jesus name.

8). Spirit of fear harassing my mind, I bury you permanently, in Jesus name.

9). I receive power from God to overthrow every fear and doubt, in Jesus name.

10).I receive power from God to overcome the spirit of anger, in Jesus name.

11). I receive the power of love to overthrow the desire to hate, in Jesus name.

12).O God, give me a humble spirit that destroys pride with ease, in Jesus name.

13).Holy Spirit anoint me with the anointing of ease, in Jesus name.

14).My Father, cause the lines to fall in perfect places for me, in Jesus name.

CHAPTER
EIGHT

Symbols of the Holy Spirit

`Studying the Old and New Testament sections of the Bible will show that a lot of imageries are used to depict persons, events and other activities. These symbols go beyond their literary forms to give deeper meanings and colorful descriptions to the characters or events they represent.

This flagrant use of symbols in the Bible literature is very useful as it helps bring to life the hidden meanings behind certain doctrines, teachings and practices that would ordinarily have been glossed over if they were in plain words, mere phrases or sentences.

In numerous Bible contexts, figurative language and other literary art forms such as parables, paradox, oxymoron, types, and metaphors are elaborately applied to Deify God, glorify Christ, symbolize the Holy Spirit or represent certain events involving them in ways beyond the ordinary meaning.

For this reason, the symbols that describe the Holy Spirit will be given detailed attention as they require some explanation for clarity and understanding. This will help bring his personality into proper perspective and explain the meaning of his figurative representation. It will also help the Christian scholar or bible teacher to understand in better ways the spiritual nature and activities of this third member of the god-head.

In this chapter, we shall take a look at some of the emblems that describe the Holy Spirit in the Bible. They include familiar, visible objects, invisible substances, and common animate and inanimate elements that reveal the Holy Spirit at work in different places and circumstances

In one case, the Holy Spirit is described as "a mighty rushing wind". Here, the Hebrew word "Rauch", which stands for the wind, breath or spirit is applied to describe him.

The word breath, which made man a living being at creation, is same as the wind that revived life in the valley of dry bones. He is the same Holy Spirit who in the form of a mighty rushing wind baptized Jesus' disciples on the day of Pentecost. He is also represented by fire, cloud, water, rain, dove and in other places.

However, while Christians are generally discouraged from delving into the mystical nature of numbers, images and symbols, because of their association with the paranormal and divinatory arts, a basic knowledge of their value is inevitable to understand the proper operation of the Holy Spirit.

This is important as many mysteries are hidden in symbols in the bible. Secrets things belong to God. But he only reveals them to those who fear him. So, by understanding these symbols, a person's perception of spiritual issues will be clearer. It will even help a believer to have a better insight into the essence of God.

Each symbol reveals a character of God in a unique way that is uncommon to the natural mind. And it is a good comprehension of them that distinguishes a serious Christian from the casual one.

When these symbols are not perceived in the context of what they represent, their full meanings are lost. So, by appreciating the properties of the substances that symbolize the Holy Spirit, we can have a better understanding of his nature and why he operates the way he does. For this reason, some of them will be discussed below.

1). **He is like the wind.**

The Holy Spirit is described in the bible as the wind. This is a fitting figure of speech because it captures his vitality, invisibility, and unpredictability. Just as the air is certain for natural survival, the presence of the Holy Spirit is inevitable for the sustenance of life.

And while the certainty of the wind's existence is not in doubt, the wind by its very nature is not perceptible to the human sight or touch. This also is the great mystery of the Holy Spirit. Thus, the nature of the wind suitably compares to the activities of the Holy Spirit.

Even meteorologists who scientifically claim to understand all the activities of the wind have several times erred in their predictions of its speed, and ultimate direction. In the same way, no human mind is able to perfectly predict the flow and behavior of the Holy Spirit, fully understand the mystery of his celestial nature, predict his direction or manipulate his actions and power.

The wind (air), like the Holy Spirit is also forever present. As it was in the Old Testament, so it is today. Like the fresh air is to the body and soul, the effect of the of the Holy Spirit in a Christian life is soothing, refreshing and comforting, thoroughly calming to the accommodating soul, even in troubled times.

In the Old Testament Hebrew Bible, the word, "Rauch", which describes wind, is equivalent to the Greek word, "Pnuemah", that defines the same phenomenon in the New Testament. The Hebrew word and its Greek counterpart mean the same thing.

So, in Both the Hebrew and Greek languages, the same word for wind is used to describe "spirit" or "breath". As the wind or air sustains physical life, so does the Holy Spirit sustain spiritual life. For he is the life-giving power of God from whom all living souls received life.

"And the earth was without form, and void; and darkness was upon the face of the deep. And the Spirit of God moved upon the face of the waters" (Genesis 1: 2).

"Behold my servant, whom I uphold; mine elect, in whom my soul delighteth; I have put my spirit upon him: he shall bring forth judgment to the Gentiles" (Isaiah 42: 1).

"And there was delivered unto him the book of the prophet Esaias. And when he had opened the book, he found the place where it was written, The Spirit of the Lord is upon me, because he hath anointed me to preach the gospel to the poor; he hath sent me to heal the brokenhearted, to preach deliverance to the captives, and recovering of sight to the blind, to set at liberty them that are bruised" (Luke 4: 17-18"

But it must be clearly understood that not every manifestation of the wind represents a move of the Holy Spirit. This is because, there can also be ordinary, natural, bulk movement of air. The scriptures describe two respective events in the Bible that serve as good illustrations here for clarity.

Two case studies that can be considered refer to experiences encountered by the Prophet Elijah at one instance and another by the Patriarch Job, on another occasion.

In the matter of prophet Elijah, when he stood by the mouth of a cave expecting the manifestation of God, observe that while the wind was implicated in the celestial rumblings that transpired, the Holy Spirit did not speak through any of the violent eruptions that occurred.

"And he said, Go forth, and stand upon the mount before the Lord. And, behold, the Lord passed by, and a great and strong wind rent the mountains, and brake in pieces the rocks before the Lord; but the Lord was not in the wind: and after the wind an earthquake; but the Lord was not in the earthquake: And after the earthquake a fire; but the Lord was not in the fire: and after the fire a still small voice. And it was so, when Elijah heard it, that he wrapped his face in his mantle, and went out, and stood in the entering in of the cave. And, behold, there came a voice unto him, and said, What doest thou here, Elijah?" (1Kings 19: 11-13).

It is clear that while there was a manifestation of strong wind, the "Lord" was not in that wind. God's still, small voice only spoke after the wind passed. So, God was not in the wind. However, in Job's astonishing experience, God spoke very clearly out of the whirlwind, in obvious response to the suffering Patriarch's boisterous arguments.

"Then the Lord answered Job out of the whirlwind, and said, Who is this that darkeneth counsel by words without knowledge? (Job 38: 1-2).

"Then answered the Lord unto Job out of the whirlwind, and said, Gird up thy loins now like a man: I will demand of thee, and declare thou unto me" (Job 40: 6).

When the Holy Spirit comes as the wind, he does so with overwhelming awe. His move upon the disciples on the day of

Pentecost is a good example of this method of his operation. On that occasion, he not only appeared as "a mighty rushing wind" but sat on each person as a glowing tongue of fire. He literally burned within their souls as he possessed their spirits and souls (Acts 2: 1-2).

The move of a mighty rushing wind is certainly an awesome sight to behold. It is also a novel experience that can change any live forever. This is that same "wind from God" which made man a living-being at creation. For sure, it certainly has inherent ability to revive the mortal man, as well as refresh and sustain any soul that sin has rendered lifeless.

This "wind" is the Spirit of God which can sweep up a wretched soul headed for hell and spin him into a new man redeemed by the blood, washed by the water of the word and surrendered to Christ in the new-birth.

2). **He is like the flame of fire.**

From the general perspective, fire is a compound made up of different gases. It serves many good purposes to mankind. While it possesses very useful potential to the advantage of humanity, it has the power to do untold damage if it is not properly handled.

It is a major source of heat, warmth and light, without which human life will altogether be boring, uncomfortable and miserable. Winter will be very dreary, most foods will spoil if not properly preserved, and night-time will be very dark and scary.

Just as fire represents positive and negative omens in the natural realm, it has the same abilities in the supernatural sphere. Its appearance on occasions in the Bible served as sign announcing the presence of God. Its most eminent appearance was on the occasion of God's call of Moses into ministry (Exodus 3: 1-4). On three instances also, God appeared to Elijah by fire.

In apostle Pauls' letter to the Hebrew believer's, he described God as a consuming fire. Only those whose sins have been consumed by God's "Holy fire" can produce fruits like Christ. So, it is surprising that fire is used to describe the presence of the Holy Spirit.

In the Old Testament Judaism, the consuming power of fire played very important role in ancient sacrificial worship. Thereafter, it continued to serve this constant, sacred purpose in most of the daily tabernacle rituals, as well as in human society.

"And it came to pass, that, when the sun went down, and it was dark, behold a smoking furnace, and a burning lamp that passed between those pieces" (Genesis 15: 17).

"And there came a fire out from before the Lord, and consumed upon the altar the burnt offering and the fat: which when all the people saw, they shouted, and fell on their faces" (Leviticus 9:24).

From the earliest records of man in antiquity, fire has played diverse roles, whether as a component for human comfort, instrument of divine worship and punishment, weapon of destruction during wars or as instrument of idol worship for human and animal sacrifices to the gods.

So, either as smoking furnace or burning lamp, it was God who lit the first fire on the sacred altar of burn offerings when he passed through Abraham's sacrifice in the form of a blazing torch (Genesis 15: 17). And through the ministry of Prophet Moses, God also charged the priests to keep the fire on his altars and in tabernacle burning continually (Leviticus 6: 13).

In the same manner, God gave the Holy Spirit to Christ's

disciples on the Day of Pentecost. This Holy Spirit is a divine gift to all believers, then and now, to indwell their hearts eternally and keeping them burning with the supernatural zeal, in continuation of Christ's righteous works.

In several outstanding events in the Bible narrative, fire accompanied God's revelation of himself to his servants. In the matter of Moses' call to ministry, for instance, God spoke to him after he turned to look at the unprecedented act of a burning bush, in which the bush was not consumed.

Again, during Israel's "exodus" out of Egypt, God led the children of Jacob by a pillar of fire by night to show them the way. But he stood as a pillar of cloud behind them, causing their stubborn, Egyptian pursuers to grope in thick darkness.

> *"And the Lord went before them by day in a pillar of a cloud, to lead them the way; and by night in a pillar of fire, to give them light; to go by day and night: He took not away the pillar of cloud by day, nor the pillar of fire by night, from before them" (Exodus 13: 21-22).*

In the spectacular contest on Mount Carmel, between Prophet Elijah and the four-hundred and fifty prophets of Baal and Asherah that served King Ahab and Jezebel, the prophet of God called down fire from heaven to consume his sacrifice. This is one clear evidence of the Holy Spirit operation in the Old Testament.

Also, when Prophet Elijah and his un-named servant were ambushed by menacing Syrian army, God sent invisible chariots of fire to protect them. This same Prophet Elijah is on record to have been transported to heaven on chariots of fire, at the end of his earthly ministry.

Thus, while the manifestation of spiritual fire is some evidence of God's supernatural presence for cleansing on one hand, it can also represent the instrument of judgment on the other. This incandescent flame of God is what is described in some scriptures as "Fire of the Lord" or "Holy Ghost fire" (Numbers 11:1; 3:2; 2 Kings 1:10-12).

It is from this perspective that certain events and persons in the Bible, who operated by the influence of this power or the outflow of it, were described as being moved by the fire of the Holy Ghost.

The Holy Spirit possesses the glowing qualities of burning flame that produces both heat and glistening light. He is the flaming "chariot of fire" that transports God and the unapproachable light that surrounds the dwelling place of the Almighty.

These physical appearances of the Holy Ghost, in the forms of cloud and fire, represent God's ever-abiding presence over his people, to guide, guard, and direct them in the path they should go.

Manifestations of this fire-nature of God occurred several places in the bible, showing how the Holy Spirit can physically appear to God's children to motivate or inspire them for exploits.

God severally appeared as fire in the congregation of his children to confirm his presence, strengthen them against temptation, ordain chosen people for service, incubate them with knowledge, endow with gifts, instruct, guide or protect his interest in their lives.

In the Old Testament, he showed up as a consuming fire, either as a sign of approval in the acceptance of their offering, as tongues of flame symbolizing holiness on some designated environment or as liquid fire of destruction to make strong statement of chastisement in rejection of transgression.

The holy Spirit is that great power that God unleashes against human or spiritual oppressors to completely subdue them. He is the fire that humiliates challenges and drowns problems (Exodus 14: 31).

This is in addition to showing-up as dazzling light to deal with his enemies or shining-light to lead, guide or directs his faithful children, either by day, night, or in desolate and lonely times, as they are walk "through the valley of shadow of death".

For his ability to accomplish these actions, he is rightly described as fire. This is because fire refines, purges, cleanses, and purifies believers from all unrighteous values and attachments to this world. And through his baptism of fire, he prepares Christians for the unavoidable life of persecution, and rejection.

The Holy Spirit is that symbol of fire who intervenes on behalf of God's kingdom, bringing the ungodly, as well as the Christian back-slider to judgment. This is the fire of judgment that visits unrighteous sons of men.

For these and many other reasons, the symbol of fire is biblically applied in describing the various incandescent manifestations of the Holy Spirit. Other forms of his fiery manifestations include:

i). **Smoking furnace and burning lamp (Genesis 15: 17).**
ii). **Brimstone and fire from heaven (Genesis 19: 24).**
iii). **Fire in the burning bush (Exodus 3: 2).**
iv). **Pillar of fire (Exodus 13: 21-22).**
v). **Cloven tongues of fire (Acts 2: 3-4).**

3). He is like the dove.

The dove is a member of the pigeon family. Both the dove and the pigeon belong to a specie of lovable birds easily domesticated for their gentle character and harmless disposition. The Holy Spirit is a humble Being with a meek and very tender personality.

Because of the affable characters of the dove, it is widely accepted by theologians and Bible students as the general symbol of peace. And that is also because doves are generally identified with calm, peace and order, which basic emotions are evoked in any life overwhelmed by the Holy Spirit.

Doves are monogamous birds by nature and each dove is known to stick with one mating partner in its life-time. This unique virtue points to their integrity, loyalty, faithfulness, devotion, optimism, and friendship. So, it is not out of place that a bird with these unique characters will be used to describe the personality of The Holy Spirit.

It is also not surprising that doves and birds in the pigeon family, were highly revered in the ancient Judaism for their sacrificial value, and importance in the Hebraic religious worship. Because, long before the Levitical rituals of the Mosaic law, the dove had featured alongside other select animals of the herd and the flock as acceptable offering approved by God for sacrificial worship.

The best-known biblical example of the dove as a ritual offering of worship, is described in God's demand that Abram provide a three-year-old heifer, a three-year-old goat, a three-year-old ram, a turtledove and a young pigeon for sacrifice.

But while all the animals were each split in the middle, (each piece lying beside the other), the dove and young pigeon where not so divided. It is important to understand that while the offering of the heifer represented God's covenant of Faith with Abraham, the sacrifice of the goat, foreshadowed God's covenant Law with Moses.

The ram (or young lamb) being symbol of Christ, however, pre-figured the age of the New Testament, while the dove and young pigeon represented the presence of Holy Spirit, which was bestowed upon all the children of faith in the post-Pentecost era (Genesis 15: 6-9).

So, even in pre-Hebrew society, these fowls were revered, and subsequently became permanent features in the Levitical sacrificial system. Doves were mythologically perceived as spirit messengers. They symbolized emblems of purity, represented instruments of holiness, and were considered as harbingers of peace.

They were readily available, easily affordable, and for the roles they played in sacred ritual worship, it was understandable why Jesus overturned the tables of those who treated them as mere merchandise, un-deserving of sacred dignity. So, from ancient times, the dove earned it reputation as a respectful symbol of the Holy Spirit.

According to the Bible narrative, the Holy Spirit of God was the instrument of divine correction who worked with God and his Word, to restore order in the midst the confusion that showed up on earth, in the wake of creation. After he brooded over the face of the earth, as a dove incubates her eggs, God spoke. At that instant, light was birth, causing darkness to rescind. Order also appeared, replacing the confusion and emptiness that dared contest with the works of God.

Also, on Mount Ararat, the dove played the role of agent of good news after the entire earth that existed at that time had been destroyed by the flood because of sin. It was after the dove that Noah sent out to survey the earth returned that he was convinced that the flood-water had receded.

After two long reconnaissance tours, the dove returned with an olive branch in its mouth. That sign alone was a symbol of hope and life. It shows the character of the dove as a credible, honest, trustworthy, and dependable partner. All the mentioned virtues are characters associated with the Holy Spirit.

During Jesus' baptism, the Bible states that the Spirit which rested on him as he came out of the water came in bodily form, like a dove. This agrees with the words of Isaiah which said,

"And the spirit of the Lord shall rest upon him, the spirit of wisdom and understanding, the spirit of counsel and might, the spirit of knowledge and of the fear of the Lord" (Isaiah 11: 2).

The dove literally behaves like the Holy Spirit in many ways. He is pure in spirit, innocent in character, of gentle disposition, faithful beyond doubt and is undefiled in nature. However, just like a dove will depart from its partner when it is betrayed, the presence of God will become far from a life that continually grieves the Holy Spirit by sinning.

It is a horrible thing to put the Holy Spirit in a situation where he has to grieve and mourn. David understood the consequence of this horrible condition. No wonder he pleaded with God after he sinned in the matter of Bathsheba, saying,

"Cast me not away from thy presence; and take not thy holy spirit from me" (Psalms 51: 1).

A believer in whom the Holy Spirit is inactive because of sin becomes spiritually useless to his church and worthless to God. Because they are useless to the kingdom of God, they are banished from the privileges such as God's divine presence, his love, counsel, wisdom, provision and the comforts of his protection.

That is why every believer's union with the Holy Spirit must be considered as inevitable. The Christian should reverently covet and guard his relationship with him by never grieving him. The Holy Spirit is a reliably partner who must be welcome with open arms.

4). He is like the rain.

The rain is another appropriate symbol that describes the nature of the Holy Spirit. This metaphor was used by Prophet

Joel about seven-hundred years before the actual "Holy Spirit, out-pouring" upon Christ's disciples became a reality. As the disciples gathered in the upper room in anticipation of the promise of the Father, on the day of Pentecost, there was an out-pouring of the Holy Spirit, which came like rain upon them.

> *"And it shall come to pass afterward, that I will pour out my spirit upon all flesh; and your sons and your daughters shall prophesy, your old men shall dream dreams, your young men shall see visions: And also upon the servants and upon the handmaids in those days will I pour out my spirit" (Joel 2: 28-29).*

> *"And it shall come to pass in the last days, saith God, I will pour out of my Spirit upon all flesh: and your sons and your daughters shall prophesy, and your young men shall see visions, and your old men shall dream dreams: And on my servants and on my handmaidens I will pour out in those days of my Spirit; and they shall prophesy" (Acts 2: 17-18).*

In all Bible scriptures, rain, water, river, and dew represent the refreshing presence of God. Each of them is associated with the expression of divine restoration, release of God's providential favors and the unlimited out-pouring of divine blessings. The denial of them is generally interpreted to mean the literal absence of the Holy Spirit.

In his absence, a Christian will experience seasons of spiritual dryness or find himself virtually in a spiritual wilderness. In this situation, he will feel weary, weak, tired and unable to pray and fast. It is in such times that a believer can appreciate the refreshing presence of the Holy Spirit.

Spiritual dryness will lead to doubt, discouragement, frustration, weakness, and disbelief. But like refreshing water, the presence of the Holy Spirit brings joy, peace, and fruitfulness. He restores life where there are signs of spiritual withering or death and reverses barrenness, whether of the spirit, soul or body.

Thus, rain in its due always represents signs of good things coming into bloom and hope of harvest. When the rain comes after a season of drought, it is regarded as good omen for restoration. As a symbol of the Holy Spirit, this shows God's concern for his creation.

As rain refreshes the human body, so does the Holy Spirit calm the spiritual nerves, the weary soul, and revives the human spirit. It is in such conditions the people of faith can dream dreams and see good visions.

But in certain situations, uncontrolled rainfall has biblically been interpreted, and rightly so, as the outpouring of God's wrath. In this guise, unrestrained rainfall coupled with ceaseless flooding and the storm, are considered as signs of divine judgment.

"For yet seven days, and I will cause it to rain upon the earth forty days and forty nights; and every living substance that I have made will I destroy from off the face of the earth. And Noah did according unto all that the Lord commanded him. And Noah was six hundred years old when the flood of waters was upon the earth. And Noah went in, and his sons, and his wife, and his sons' wives with him, into the ark, because of the waters of the flood. Of clean beasts, and of beasts that are not clean, and

> *of fowls, and of everything that creepeth upon*
> *the earth, There went in two and two unto*
> *Noah into the ark, the male and the female,*
> *as God had commanded Noah. And it came*
> *to pass after seven days, that the waters of the*
> *flood were upon the earth. In the six hundredth*
> *year of Noah's life, in the second month, the*
> *seventeenth day of the month, the same day*
> *were all the fountains of the great deep broken*
> *up, and the windows of heaven were opened"*
> *(Genesis 7: 4, 11).*

Theologians also have interpreted long absence of rain in a nation or upon a people as obvious indication of ungodliness, transgression and therefore penalty for rebellion to God's laws. So, one can expect catastrophic consequences when God withdraws his rain from a nation.

Consider the drought and famine ravaged period when King Ahab ruled in Israel. The wicked king married a foreign woman called Jezebel, who worshiped pagan deities of Baal and Asherah. And at some point, Jezebel began to kill God's prophets who refused to serve his idols. So, many of the surviving prophets ran away to hide in caves. This was the horrible time of godlessness in the nation of Israel, until God sent prophet Elijah.

At prophet Elijah's command, the heavens over Israel were sealed for a period of three and a half years. During this entire period there was no rain or dew. This harsh drought resulted in a disastrous famine in Israel, for which reason several people and livestock perished.

All rivers and brooks dried up as the land became unproductive for three and half years. This was so, until Prophet Elijah reappeared at the prompting of God. And after a hotly contested spiritual battle on Mount Carmel, Jezebel's evil prophets are defeated. Thereafter, Prophet Elijah calls on God and he sends abundant rain upon the land of Israel

Rain is a sign of the refreshing work of the Holy Spirit. In the absence of the Holy Spirit, spiritual life withers. But there is abundant harvest where he dwells. So, not only does rain possess cleansing and refreshing power, it operates like the Holy Spirit by quenching the thirsty spirit and renewing the weary mind. This is how the Holy Spirit treats the Christian.

5). **He flows like a river.**

Another wonderful symbol of the Holy Spirit is the "River". Jesus used both river and water interchangeably as metaphors in speaking about the Holy Spirit. He said that the Holy Spirit within a believer, shall be like "rivers of living water".

Some bodies of water are stagnant and lifeless, but others flow freely. The free-flowing rivers support life and are purer than the standing pools. The Holy Spirit is comparable to flowing water. He flows eternally, without restraint, and cannot be obstructed.

Both the Holy Spirit and Christ work in harmony to produce fruit-bearing believers for the kingdom of God. In one of Jesus' earliest teachings in the Temple at Jerusalem, he employed this symbol to allude to the Messiah's life-giving blessings and the eternal power the coming Holy Spirit will bring.

> *"In the last day, that great day of the feast, Jesus stood and cried, saying, If any man thirst, let him come unto me, and drink. He that believeth on me, as the scripture hath said, out of his belly shall flow rivers of living water. (But this spake he of the Spirit, which they that believe on him should receive: for the Holy*

Ghost was not yet given; because that Jesus was not yet glorified" (John 7: 37-39).

This invitation to drink from "rivers of living waters" referred to the Holy Spirit who possessed the power to witness for Christ. Christ spoke of the Spirit's ability to offer eternal life to all who will believe in Jesus as the Messiah. This is the current work of the Holy Spirit and what he will continue to do till Christ's return for his church.

In whomever the Holy Spirit dwells, he brings new life, bodily refreshment, fruitfulness, power, and healing. His presence represents the picture of God's spiritual blessings flowing like a river from Christians, who have received the gifts of the Holy Spirit, to the world.

Whether as river or rain, the Holy Spirit is that refreshing water of life that flows into a believer's life when he feels tired, parched, lifeless, empty, and very thirsty. He is the refreshing power that gives new life and revives the soul. Wherever he is, he makes a difference by changing lives and bringing them to Christ.

He is the river that nourished and sustained the tree of life in the Garden of Eden in the very beginning. At that time, Adam and Eve were forbidden from eating of the fruit of this tree. However, those who overcome till the end will have still have access to this tree.

The Holy Spirit symbolizes this flowing and living river. He represents the "clear river of water of life". This is that river that is clear as crystal, which proceeds from the throne of God and of the Lamb. In the end, those who believe in Christ will drink from this river of the water of life.

The river protects the tree of life. And when the new heaven and the new earth are revealed, overcomers will freely eat from this tree and drink of this river of life. But only whose sins have been cleansed by the blood of the Lamb would qualify to drink from this river which guarantees eternal life.

6). **He is like a seal.**

A). The Holy Spirit acts as a seal in a covenant arrangement. Every covenant has four parts.

1) The parties involved.
2) The conditions of the covenant.
3) The benefits/penalties.
4) The seal. A seal is a device that joins two or more things together. It is an inevitable component of any covenant.

So, the Holy Spirit serves as the spiritual stamp that authenticates the covenant promises between God and any one or more parties. He is the instrument that confers spiritual approval on the provisions of God's agreement with man and the final evidence of consensus to the negotiation.

In the secular world, a document sealed with red wax, and on which an authorized design is embossed, is generally accepted as legal tender. This document is considered as official agreement and remains in force while the parties involved are alive. It may even expire, based on the terms of the agreement.

But a sacred covenant has more authority than an agreement. This is because blood is used as the seal, instead of red wax. This is what confers an eternal character on a covenant. The blood is the evidence that the accord is eternal, secure, binding, irrevocable, and cannot be annulled.

B). It is the vital role of the Holy Spirit to stamp believers in Christ with the symbolic evidence of their salvation. With this seal in place, the devil cannot contest those believers' confession of faith, as it confers the privilege of special possession by Christ on them. Thus, they become the "touch not" of Christ.

The Holy Spirit also acts as a seal to the believer's salvation experience. Jesus paid the price for the believer's redemption by shedding his blood on the cross at Calvary. In the Old Testament era, forgiveness of sins was sought for and obtained by shedding animal blood. But the gift of redemption which the Christian received is different.

It was procured through the shedding of human and not animal blood, following the sacrificial death of the righteous Son of God, on the cross at Calvary. However, while the blood of Jesus points the way of redemption through the forgiveness of sins, it is the Holy Spirit that stamps the redeemed with the sacred seal of adoption into the family of God. So, the seal of the Holy Spirit confers greater authority to the Christian than the blood of animals did on those who sought forgiveness in the Old Testament.

> *"Now he which stablished us with you in Christ, and anointed us, is God. Who hath also sealed us, and given the earnest of the Spirit in our hearts" (2 Corinthians 1: 21-22).*

He is the seal that identifies a Christian as someone chosen of God. He is also the guarantor of every believer's blood-redemption; and the person who authenticates his salvation experience and approves whatever requests he makes of his privileges in Christ. He distinguishes Christians for spiritual gifts, marks them as ambassadors of Christ, links them in fellowship with God and singles them out for recognition at the throne of grace.

By this seal, the Holy Spirit places a mark of protection on Christians, guiding them in the way of God. He is the sign of a believer's faithfulness, stamp of God's unfailing promises to those predestined according to divine purpose. And his indwelling presence a legitimate symbol of God's adoption and evidence of Christ's possession of that soul.

This holy signature is a genuine validation of the believer's election, particularly that Christian that is zealous for Christ on earth and is anxiously looking forward to gathering with the saints at the marriage supper of the Lamb, when Christ returns for his church.

7). **He operates like oil.**

In the Bible Old Testament era, pure olive oil was God's choice material for consecrating his chosen servants. It was used for sanctifying articles of worship. Prophets, priests, as well as kings were all anointed, as evidence of divine approval. Thus, began the reference to the worship-grade oil, as "anointing oil".

Temple furniture, garments, preparation vessels, sweet incense, grain offerings, and wafers for sacred worship were usually anointed with special oil before using them for worship. A person divinely appointed for sacred service, had his head anointed with oil and was considered as a very special agent of God. Such persons were also mightily used to the glory of God.

> *"The Spirit of the Lord is upon me, because he hath anointed me to preach the gospel to the poor; he hath sent me to heal the brokenhearted, to preach deliverance to the captives, and recovering of sight to the blind, to set at liberty them that are bruised" (Luke 4: 18).*

So, generally, oil for consecration is referred to as "Holy oil". The title "Holy", identifies with its purity, concerning the sacred purposes the oil served, especially in the holy temples and in the religious worship.

In ancient Old Testament Judaism, special olive oil produced from the olive groves of the land of Israel, was an essential component of certain grain offerings and for keeping the flame of the Menorah burning constantly. The Menorah is the seven-arm, ancient, Hebrew lamp-stand, hammered out of a chunk of pure gold.

Jewish oral mythology teaches that special olive oil was responsible for the defeat of the Greeks (Seleucids) by the Maccabees during their revolt to recover the Temple which had been vandalized. The Maccabees (group of Jewish warriors) rebelled against the Seleucid-Greeks and took control of Judea and Jerusalem, when it was under the control of the Seleucid Empire. During that revolt, the Maccabees were said to have fashioned a makeshift lampstand (Menorah), but could only find one flask of pure, temple-grade oil to keep it burning.

> *"And the Lord spake unto Moses, saying, Command the children of Israel, that they bring unto thee pure oil olive beaten for the light, to cause the lamps to burn continually"*
> *(Leviticus 24: 1-2)*

This flask of oil could only have been sufficient for a day's use. However, records by some Hebrew scholar's state that by some divine intervention, it lasted for eight days, allowing enough time to produce, pure, uncontaminated, temple- standard oil. Only the Holy Spirit could have kept that lamp burning. God is light and cannot dwell in darkness.

For this reason, "the miracle of light" is observed every Chanukah (Re-dedication of the Holy Temple) as a memorial to the victory of good over evil. So, just as God's special oil provides fuel for the constant light in the Tabernacle and later in the Temple, the Holy Spirit keeps the light of God permanently burning in a believer's soul. He is the unquenchable light that enables the believer to shine as "light" in a dark world.

Oil also plays a great role in healing process in the body. It represents the healing power of God and serves as base for compounding most healing balms and ointments. The Holy spirit is the oil that soothes the heart when it is broken by pain, grief and agony of life.

> *"But a certain Samaritan, as he journeyed, came where he was: and when he saw him, he had compassion on him, And went to him, and bound up his wounds, pouring in oil and wine, and set him on his own beast, and brought him to an inn, and took care of him" (Luke 10: 33-34).*

> *"How God anointed Jesus of Nazareth with the Holy Ghost and with power: who went about doing good, and healing all that were oppressed of the devil; for God was with him" (Acts 10: 38).*

Oil is therefore, a perfect representation of the Holy Spirit. For it meets the unique requirements for enthroning kings, consecrating priests, conferring authority on believers, bringing healing, deliverance, prosperity, and keeping the light of God aglow.

When the Holy oil of God is on a person's head, the person increasingly reflects the power of divine grace and excels in several areas of life. Many such people find pleasure and fulfillment in serving God. A believer anointed with the Holy Oil is highly honored. His word is generally respected, and because he speaks as the oracle of God, his words always come to pass.

The oil of God brings positive supernatural inspiration for

knowledge and wisdom. And this can only be attributed to the influence of the Holy Spirit. No disciple in the kingdom of God will bear useful fruit or last in ministry without his prior anointing. For it is the fresh oil of God's Holy Spirit that can keep a Christian shinning like God's light.

8). **He is like wine.**

From ancient times, wine has been a component of sacred religious worship. It was used in primitive times in ceremonies for the worship local gods and for the purpose of making libations. It also serves as an element in Christian holy sacrament. This explains its envious role in religious celebrations.

Melchizedek was an ancient Canaanite figure and the first person to be referred to as priest in the Hebrew Bible. By the Mosaic law, only descendants of Aaron qualified to be priests. However, this Melchizedek, as King of Salem and High Priest, existed before the Law of Moses, thus superseding the priesthood of Aaron.

During Melchizedek's reception of Abraham, following his victory over the five Canaanites Kings and the rescue of his nephew Lot, this Priest and King (King of Salem) offered bread and wine in the worship of God Most-High. He then blessed Abraham, from whom also he received tithes (Genesis 14: 18-20).

Through-out the Old Testament Judaism, wine played invaluable role in the religious ceremonies of the Hebrews. It also played significant roles in the socio-cultural life of their society. Thus, the importance of wine in religious practice, as well as social life of the people in ancient times and during the Old Testament bible era cannot be understated.

During Jesus days in ministry, he spoke of wine as a symbol of his blood. In this way, he gave his disciples a glimpse of the sin-cleansing power of the blood of Jesus. In Christian Holy communion, wine represents the pure and undefiled blood of Jesus that was shed for the remission of sins.

However, while the Bible submits that wine makes the heart of man merry, Nazarites were completely forbidden from drinking wine. These were people who set themselves apart for a period to fulfill special religious rites. And according to the Law of Moses also, Priests were prohibited from consuming wine or any strong drinks, prior to going into the tabernacle or temple.

The Bible compares the effect of wine to the bite of a serpent and the sting of an adder, which can result in delusions and impaired decisions. And many destines have been destroyed because of their reckless pursuit for alcoholic excitement.

In most religious as well as cultural practices, wine is considered a source of happiness, recognized in sacred worship and is used for healing purposes. But the feeling of happiness derived through alcoholic intoxication can never compare to the supernatural delight experienced from being drunk in the Holy Spirit.

While alcohol may provide its normal but temporary excitement, as is usual with most stimulants, drunkenness no sooner leaves its victims stupefied, scoffing, out-of-control, riotous, and in regrettable, unwholesome-condition of mental and physical stupor.

The real joy of the Lord comes from being filled with the Holy Spirit, which positive effects prompt a celebration in psalms, hymns and spiritual songs of thanksgiving and praise that lead to a deeper fellowship with God.

"And be not drunk with wine, wherein is excess; but be filled with the Spirit; Speaking to yourselves in psalms and hymns and spiritual

songs, singing and making melody in your heart to the Lord; Giving thanks always for all things unto God and the Father in the name of our Lord Jesus Christ" (Ephesians 5:18-20).

Worldly alcohol is a mocker that has destroyed many destinies. It is a deceiver reserved for the heathen, the foolish and those on the path of self-destruction. But a life filled with the Holy Spirit overflows in the supernatural graces of God as seen in the exuberant celebration by that Christian.

So, until a person is born of the water and the Holy Spirit, his unregenerate soul cannot experience real joy. Such creatures remain permanently attached to their trespasses, bound by the chains of debauchery, void of prudent intention and lacking in good counsel.

For this reason, believers should covet the drunkenness in the Holy Spirit. It is only in this condition that Christians can experience eternal joy, real gladness, overflowing peace and Christlike-boldness. This is the state of mind that can conquer sin and enable victorious Christian living.

9). He is like a cloud.

The cloud is a visible mass of condensed water formed above in the firmament where it holds the hope of rain. While thick dark clouds have been interpreted to be omens for gloom, and disaster, some clouds in the bible have been interpreted to mean the presence of God and the move of the Holy Spirit.

"And it came to pass, when the priests were come out of the holy place, that the cloud filled the house of the Lord, So that the priests could not stand to minister because of the cloud: for the glory of the

Lord had filled the house of the Lord. Then spake Solomon, The Lord said that he would dwell in the thick darkness" (1 Kings 8: 10-12).

"He smote also all the firstborn in their land, the chief of all their strength. He brought them forth also with silver and gold: and there was not one feeble person among their tribes. Egypt was glad when they departed: for the fear of them fell upon them. He spread a cloud for a covering; and fire to give light in the night. The people asked, and he brought quails, and satisfied them with the bread of heaven. He opened the rock, and the waters gushed out; they ran in the dry places like a river. For he remembered his holy promise, and Abraham his servant (Psalm 105: 36-42).

In these situations, these unmistakable evidence of unusual and un-natural manifestations of the cloud, physically revealed God's presence to his people. This often occurred to the Israelites as they gathered for worship in the Tabernacle or journeyed through the wilderness to the land of Canaan.

Here, the cloud is seen as a weapon of protection which God spread over Moses and his foot-army as a covering. When Moses went up the mountains to receive the tablets of the Law from God, a cloud of divine glory enveloped him. And this cloud often stood over the tabernacle and filled God's house, whenever the Children of Israel worshipped God.

The spiritual cloud also represents the divine vehicle for supernatural transportation. As the psalmist says:

"Who layeth the beams of his chambers in the waters: who maketh the cloud his chariot: who walketh upon the wings of the wind" (Psalm 104:3).

This special cloud often served God's purposes. God spoke through it when it overshadowed the atmosphere on the day of Jesus' baptism by the Jordan River. It manifested during Jesus transfiguration and also on the event of his ascension. These "cloud of evidences" were respective confirmations of the presence of the Holy Spirit on all these sacred occasions.

However, it must be noted that not every cloud, strong wind, or fire, represents the presence of the Holy Spirit. The psalmist reminds us that the dark places, which supposedly include some natural-phenomena, are full of the haunts of wickedness.

10). **He shines like light.**

Light is one of the many poetic forms in scripture that describes the active presence of God amidst his children. The carnal man on his own has no light in him but dwells in darkness. The Holy Spirit is that revered channel through whom God reflects the light of God's presence to other people, and nations.

After the Holy Spirit brooded over the earth when it was without form, empty and darkness ruled the earth, God spoke, and light manifested at his command. The Holy Spirit is the agent of the un-approachable light in which God dwells. There can be no satanic darkness wherever he is. He is the light through whom all believers see God's light.

He is the symbol of the divine light and the radiant glory that illuminates the vast the vast galaxies, dispelling fear and gloom. His fluorescence causes the sun, moon and stars that decorate the firmament to glow, shine and glitter, foreshadowing the brightness of heaven where no darkness dwells.

The Holy Spirit represents the brightness of the sun in the firmament that divides the day from the night. He is God's everlasting brightness that will never set or wane. When the scripture declares that "God rides in the dark clouds", it must be understood that even the darkest cloud before God, is brighter than any natural, shimmering light.

Through the Holy Spirit, the light of God pierces into the dark soul of the sinful man. In the way, he exposes the evil thoughts, unrighteous imaginations, demonic schemes and intents of all men, and convicts them of their sins, righteousness and judgment. It is through him that this work is accomplished.

The Holy Spirit is the agent that sustains the lamp of God even in the sinful souls that say there is no God. He lives in every man keeping his lamp glowing as man's last hope of finding his way back to God. King Solomon, in his confirmation of this truth declared that:

"The Spirit of man is the candle of the Lord searching all the inward parts of the belly" (Proverbs 20: 27).

Just as darkness is generally used to imply falsehood, "Light" symbolizes the truth and all that is good. God's light is the source and power of great virtues such as wisdom, knowledge, understanding, revelation, and vision. And that light, is the Holy Spirit.

He is the light of the gospel of grace from whom shines the sun of righteousness, Jesus Christ, the Son of the living God. He is not a feeble, or gloomy light, but the brightness of the unapproachable sun. He is the light of life and the light which gives life to all men. Without his light, nothing can come to life and nothing living can survive.

Jesus refers to believers as the light of the world. As true light, he expects that believers in whom dwells the Spirit of God will go forth and shine brightly, in a world overshadowed by demonic cloud of darkness. He goes further to say:

> *"Let your light so shine before men, that they may see your good works and glorify your father in heaven" (Matthew 5: 16).*

The shining light of a child of faith impacts his world positively to the glory of God. Those Christian's have tremendous urge to please God in whatever they do. As such, they do not compromise their faith by condoning any measure of evil and have no communion with the workers of iniquity.

Holy Spirit-filled believers shine with convincing, shimmering light. Such Christians abound in good works, grow readily in righteousness, wisdom and knowledge, and win souls for the kingdom of God to the delight of heaven. This is great testimony to Christ's life and ministry made possible by the light of the Holy Spirit.

PRAYER POINTS.

1). Life-giving wind of God blow upon my dry bones, in Jesus name.

2). Wind of God, bring fortune from the ends of the earth into my life, in Jesus name.

3). Wind of life, revive my spirit, in Jesus name.

4). Word of the living God, burn in my bones like fire, in Jesus name.

5). Fire of God enter my foundation and destroy every filth there, in Jesus name.

6). Fire of God enter my father's house and destroy every idol there, in Jesus name.

7). Fire of God enter my mother's house and destroy all evil altars there, in Jesus name.

8). O God, use me as your instrument of peace, in Jesus name.

9). Rain of divine favor soak my life from head to the soles of my feet, in Jesus name.

10). River of life, flow into my life and family, in Jesus name.

11). River of general prosperity, flow into my life, in Jesus name.

12). Blood of Jesus, seal my life divine opportunities, in Jesus name.

13). Oil of God, heal me where I need healing, in Jesus name.

14). O Lord, make me drunk with the wine of the Holy Spirit, in Jesus name.

NINE

Gifts of the Holy Spirit

Every Christian deserves to operate in the gifts of the Holy Spirit. But these gifts have to be desired. The is because, God delights in manifesting himself to the world through those who honor him. And his acts can only be replicated through people who are filled with his spirit.

Every gift has its worth. But some gifts have greater value than others because of their source. That is why spiritual gifts from God are considered as very precious treasures. God gives these gifts to his children for the greater benefit of the church in particular and the world at large. It is a divine privilege and a thing of great honor to be a recipient of God's gift.

Thus, God's gifts are special treasures because they are from his divine source. So, it is very important that they are used to the benefit of God's people. The Holy Spirit is the spiritual means through whom the divine gifts manifest to the church and he teaches how they should be employed to the glory of God.

Sadly, only a small number of believers know this aspect of the Holy Spirit and how he operates. Worst still, even fewer believers acknowledge that the Holy Spirit exists. This explains why not many Christians have received his baptism which enables the recipients to live and operate in the power of his gifts.

How tragic that many Christians will live their entire lifetime without experiencing intimate fellowship with the Holy Spirit. And how dangerous for any believer to operate in life and ministry without the power of the Holy Spirit. But this can happen out of ignorance, lack of wisdom or wrong teaching.

He is the power that sustains the church. So, his absence due to sin or ignorance is an indication of danger for the body of Christ. For without his presence, the body of Christ is weak and vulnerable to the enemy. Thus, the Holy Spirit must not only be present but have the freedom and sound environment to operate.

When the apostle Paul encountered a group of disciples in Ephesus who honestly confessed that they never heard if there was any Holy Ghost, he understood their innocence and predicament. They were only exposed to the baptism of "John the Baptist", which taught about forgiveness that comes by repentance from sins.

"He said unto them. Have ye received the Holy Ghost since ye believed? And they said unto him. We have not so much as heard whether there be any Holy Ghost. And he said unto them, Unto what then were ye baptized? And they said, Unto John's baptism" (Acts 19: 2-3).

So, the Apostle Paul taught them about the Holy Spirit and his gifts. And when he had explained all things to them, he baptized them in the name of the Lord Jesus Christ. Thereafter, he laid hands upon these Ephesian-believers and the Holy Ghost came upon them.

This teaches that the baptism of apostle John is only a step in the process of conversion. But while it is vital, it only stops at cleansing human sin. But this is not sufficient to initiate a convert into the kingdom's ministerial service. Such a Christian was only as good as a soldier in the military camp who needed to prove himself in training before he could be trusted with weapons for battle-field experience.

Those Ephesians had the zeal to serve in the kingdom of God but were deficient in power to face real battles. This is a dangerous place to be concerning spiritual issues. That is why the baptism of the Holy Spirit, which equips Christians with the gifts for ministry and warfare, is inevitable in a believer's life.

Consider the case of the Apostle Apollos too. He was an eloquent Jewish-born, Christian preacher and a contemporary of Paul the Apostle. Though he was learned and competent in the Old Testament scriptures and taught accurately of things concerning Jesus, he was only versed in the doctrine of John's baptism as well (Acts 18: 23-28).

But when Aquila and Priscilla, two more seasoned disciples of Jesus heard him preaching in Ephesus, they took him aside and more accurately, explained "the way of God" to him. That it did not only require repentance from sins, but also involved the belief in Christ, the perfect life he lived and the significance of his death, resurrection and ascension. All these great events were made possible by the intervention of the Holy Spirit.

Although Apollos was fervent in the spirit, his zealous ministrations were based mainly on his human oratorial skills. His understanding of Jesus' entire life and ministry was deficient, and he did not know about the coming of the Holy Spirit. But after his knowledge was made more complete, God mightily used him to strengthen the body of Christ.

Lack of knowledge or mis-understanding of these basic elements of the Christian faith will leave cracks in the foundations of believer's doctrinal beliefs. Such flaws deny Christians vital benefits reserved for people of faith. But with a deeper understanding of biblical doctrines, like Apollos received, a convert becomes a better instrument in the hand of the Holy Spirit to strengthen and encourage the church.

It is thus unimaginable that any Christian will defraud himself of the invaluable gifts of the Holy Spirit. These are privileges tied to a person's conversion experience and are just once crucial step away. It is thus very tragic that Christians do not possess them or are deny themselves of these vital rights due to ignorance, heresy or doctrinal divisions in the church.

The Holy Spirit exists, and he is God's instrument for anointing the church with power. Through his gifts, Christians are transformed for ministry and enabled to bear Christ-like fruit. His gifts make the difference in a life that has accepted Christ as Lord and Savior. For without those gifts, the Christian is weak in all areas of life and ministry.

Apostle Paul was a man perceived to be weak in physical appearance. But even his critics confirmed that his words resonated with spiritual wisdom and power. This was because he was totally surrendered to Christ and was completely possessed by God's Spirit.

The spiritual gifts we will consider in this chapter are from God the Father who offers gifts without finding faults. They are conferred by God to enable extra-ordinary abilities in the lives of ordinary, natural Christians. They are not gifts possessed by merit, neither are they received because they are deserved but represent the power of God which distinguishes committed believers from the pack of church-bench warmers. This latter group may be born-again but lack the hunger for divine power.

Pastor Kenneth E. Hagin, in his book, "Gifts of the Spirit", draws a distinction between God's providential blessings for everyone (believers and unbelievers alike) and the gifts that come from the Holy Spirit, which are specially reserved for the church and Christians.

What this means is that there are general blessings conferred on the earth for the benefit of all mankind. However, there are special gifts for kingdom service. These special gifts represent divine abilities reserved only for special people, which he confers upon them at the time they are baptized with the Holy Spirit.

Unfortunately, many believers do not receive these gifts. Either due to ignorance regarding the real nature of the godhead, lack of love and spiritual passion for the things of Christ or a limited understanding in issues that matter to God. Any of these will put the Holy Spirit and his benefits out of a person's spiritual reach.

The consequence is that only a small segment of the Christian community has any good knowledge about the Holy Spirit and his gifts. The rest scarcely know who he is, what his gifts are, why they were given, how they can be received, their benefits and the best means of exploiting these divine gifts.

However, the modern-day Church can learn a lot through the epistles of the Apostle Paul. He was a man incredibly overwhelmed by the presence of divine glory and humbled by the transforming power of the Holy Spirit. And the gifts of the Holy Spirit empowered him in very unique ways that he ministered with un-equaled power and boldness.

The influence of the Holy Spirit inspires believers beyond measure, helping them adopt a positive attitude to whatever circumstances they face. And it keeps them calm in tough situations. This was true for the life of the great Apostle Paul. Through these gifts, he persevered in all situations and received strength that enabled him to operate outside the limited scope of human perception.

Nobody can succeed in life or be useful in God's kingdom-matters without the help of the Holy Spirit. His gifts motivate Christians in their effort to fulfill their God-inspired dreams. And it is a very great honor to be endowed with the precious treasures and incredible power of the Holy Spirit.

The gifts of the Holy Spirit to the church community are a tacit affirmation of God's image in his children. They represent spiritual power on an individual on whom such presents have been bestowed and further signify the evidence of unity in the body of Christ.

These supernatural expressions of God's power through his children can manifest in unitary form. But sometimes, a person can be endowed with more than one gift. In that case, the gifts will operate in combination. But in which-ever manner they manifest, they work in orderly manner, in unity and never contradict each other.

Moses was a man abundantly filled with God's Spirit. He was so rich in the gifts of God that when God passed on the gracious spirit of prophecy from Moses to seventy selected elders of Israel, they all prophesied in the camp as God gave them unction.

The primary function of all spiritual gifts is to empower believers for kingdom service. This is God objective in giving these gifts to his children. The different gifts operate in diversities of ways, but are given by the same Spirit, who divides to everyone as the Spirit wills.

Bible scholars generally agree that there are nine major gifts of the Holy Spirit. These gifts all belong to the Church and are manifested through Christians for the Church, as the Spirit of God determines.

In general, all the nine major gifts of the Holy Spirit are described as manifestation gifts. This is because, they represent the various ways through which God reveals himself to the church.

The present-day church needs these gifts as in the early days of the church history when the disciples vibrated with God's power. The reason there are no more great moves of God's power in the present Church age is because Christians are empty of the Holy Spirit.

The modern Church needs this power as in the early days of the Apostles. Without the power, Christian prayer altars will be weak, and the believers will be at risk of becoming prey to the powers of darkness. But as the gifts of God are demonstrated in the church, the enemy will fear God and flee from his children.

The nine gifts of the Holy Spirit are classified into three groups in the bible, each group with three sub-heads based on their mode of operations. They include:

The manifestation gifts.

The manifestation gifts refer to those acts of which the Holy Spirit through a physical being, which enable that Christian to manifest with supernatural abilities. They are gifts to the Church, through the Holy Spirit reveals spiritual things the mind of God. They include:

1). The revelation gifts.

Revelation gifts represent three different dimensions of God's character:

i). Word of knowledge.

By general definition, knowledge represents a deep familiarity with facts. It describes an awareness of a body of principles, an acquaintance with a place or deep understanding of a thing grasped by the mind. It also represents facts that are accumulated by learning.

But from spiritual perspective, knowledge includes the comprehension of the body of truths which exist even though the natural mind may not perceive them. It is the understanding of mysteries that exist beyond the natural sphere, which the limited human mind cannot comprehend except by supernatural intervention.

Fools resist knowledge and even when it is from God, they despise his means to it, disdain his counsel, and mock divine corrections to their own peril. Unknown to them, it is the fear of God that leads to knowledge which he gives to steer the wise away from pain and anguish. But the complacency of fools brings destruction into their lives.

When knowledge is from God, it helps a person to live well and right. So, to know what God desires and not what the world demands, and to live strictly by them is what delights the heart of God. It is a gift of the Holy Spirit and evidence of his manifestation in a believer.

Thus, the "Gift of the Word of knowledge" denotes the spiritual ingenuity that enables a Christian to understand in part or have some mental grasp of supernatural issues in certain times. It helps in the understanding of matters which to others remain mysteries and keep them in the dark except the Holy Spirit intervenes.

It is a divine supernatural impartation given to people that are intimate with God. And though this intimacy stems from regular study of the Bible, meditation on God's word, ceaseless prayer, regular fasting, and an honest and passionate desire to serve in God's kingdom, it is not a guarantee for receiving the gift.

The gift of word of knowledge is the outpouring of a measure of spiritual thoughts from the mind of God. It is the release of divine information, data, and indisputable truth into the natural mind, for the benefit of the church. By this gift, the natural man gains insight into some aspects, but not all of the hidden thoughts of God.

"For to one is given by the Spirit the word of wisdom; to another the word of knowledge by the same Spirit" (1 Corinthians 12: 8).

This gift equips those who possess it to clearly understand in a particular time and place, what God desires to be passed on to the church. And it also helps to understand how knowing the will of God can be followed by the strict leading of his Spirit in accomplishing his instructions.

The reason this endowment is described as **"Gift of the word of knowledge"** and not **"Gift of knowledge"**, is because it is only a partial supernatural insight (through visions, dreams, and revelations) into the thoughts of God. Referring to this gift as "the gift of knowledge", would have implied the impartation of the entire thoughts of God to man, which feat is not possible.

Every man's best carnal intelligence, worldly wisdom and understanding of things in this natural realm is insufficient to help him or his society to navigate through life with less challenges. And in a fallen world that is littered with all manner of deceptions, evil pit-falls and satanic snares that lead to confusion, people are bound to regularly take the wrong turns in the journey of life.

But by operating of the gift of the word of knowledge, the church can overcome any such difficulties. That is why God gives his children the gift of "Word of knowledge" so that children of God can know the right path to follow and avoid problems.

An example of the manifestation of the Gift of the word of knowledge is seen in story taken from the Gospel of Matthew. When Jesus asked his disciples, "whom say ye that I am?" None of them came up with any answer, until Peter said, "Thou art the Christ, the Son of the living God". Jesus explained right there to Peter that his response could only have been revealed to him by

God. So, Apostle Peter manifested in this gift even before the Holy Spirit was revealed to the church. (Matthew 16: 15-17).

It is a great privilege to know the divine thoughts of God. It serves as light in the darkness and helps the believer understand what appears to other simple minds as mystery. But note that while a person may experience frequent manifestations of this gift, it cannot be accumulated, gained by human efforts or acquired by learning. This gift is different from the gift of discernment which describes the ability to see what God has shown or revealed.

ii). **Word of wisdom.**

Word of Wisdom is the ability to apply the knowledge acquired from God in a timely and proper manner. It is a divine gift endowed by the Holy Spirit for the work of ministry and for edifying the body of Christ. Even in the Old Testament, God chose wise and skillful artisans whom he filled with this gift for service in his Holy Tabernacle (Exodus 28: 3).

He is still doing the same today, choosing and filling believers hearts, with the Spirit of God in knowledge, in understanding and in wisdom. This wisdom is the ability to properly and timely exploit what is known. It is a spiritual gift reserved mainly only for people of faith who humbly yield themselves as vessels through whom God can flow to the community of his children.

A believer's expertise, skill, and talent can only be useful for kingdom service when it is impacted by the Holy Spirit. So, this wisdom is an invaluable spiritual asset that a believer should covet. Joshua excelled in this gift as well as King Solomon. Every Christian requires some level of wisdom to succeed in life. Such is its value that people like King Solomon looked unto God for it because he understood its indispensable value.

King Solomon seriously desired it. He prayed to God for it and was rewarded. For God gave him this gift above measure and in every facet of life. God is still generously offering the same spiritual gift in this age to those who earnestly ask him. He still willingly gives it to all who are ready to apply it for his kingdom sake.

> *"If any of you lack wisdom, let him ask of God, that giveth to all men liberally, and upbraideth not; and it shall be given him" (James 1: 5).*

The bible stresses the need to possess this gift. And those who are endowed with it are expected to use it with great understanding and humility. By using this gift of the word of wisdom, believers can advance the cause of Christ, bring honor to his Church, and glory to the name of God.

> *"Wisdom is the principal thing; therefore get wisdom: and with all thy getting get understanding" (Proverbs 4: 7).*

A mind that is saturated with the word of God will ultimately overflow with the power of divine wisdom. Godly wisdom is a spiritual tool of defense. With it, the Holy Spirit distinguishes God's purpose for his children, protecting their lives from the foolish agenda of the devil by which he rules in this dark world. (Ecclesiastes 7: 11-12).

A word from God becomes useless to the Church if not timely and properly applied. It is not enough to know a godly truth. What matters is how, and when it is applied to the benefit of the body of Christ and the society at large. That is how important this gift is in the life of a Christian.

Consider the exchange between the suffering Patriarch Job and his friend Elihu who had come to console him. While Elihu rightly submitted that God alone was the source of real wisdom, his intended counsel in this situation, did not bring any succor to the suffering Job.

It is important in the application of godly-wisdom to focus on brightening the counselee's hope. Wise counsel should lift the faith of the downcast and not cause him to hurt more. It should involve wise words of encouragement that strengthen the weak in spirit. This will inspire the broken-hearted to pick-up the pieces while still looking onto God.

A Christian who is unable to properly utilize this gift is at best a literate fool or a spiritual accident looking for where to happen. He is not only a hazard to the Church but a harmful tool to his community and a danger to himself. Misuse of this gift will lead many suffering Christians of weak conscience to backslide.

iii). **Discerning of spirits.**

The "Gift of Discernment" or "Discerning of spirits" is one great way in which the Holy Spirit operates. If the church can operate correctly in this gift, many Christians will be saved from the activity of false prophets and teachers. A lot of imitation of this gift operates in many spiritual communities today. And the deception created by this fake spirituality has led many gullible and "carnal-minded" Christians astray.

> *"Now the Spirit speaketh expressly, that in the latter times some shall depart from the faith, giving heed to seducing spirits, and doctrines of devils;" (1 Timothy 4: 1).*

This gift is of exceeding value and is given to edify the body of Christ. But it can be misinterpreted, misapplied, and seriously misunderstood. Because, just as God is revealing himself to humanity, the Devil is busy doing the same. So, it now requires spiritual sanity to differentiate between what a person perceives and its source to make useful meaning and not misconstrue this gift as the ability to see spirits, which it is not.

The Christian must therefore be very careful not to confuse the gift to Discern spirits with clairvoyance, hallucination, or psychic abilities, all of which are different satanic forms of seeing, hearing or mentally grasping activities happening in the invisible realm.

Although our modern society is neck deep in spiritism, excited with magic, and openly engages in witchcraft, the Christian who cherishes his authority in Christ is forbidden from dabbling into any form of mysticism under the pretext of seeking the gift of discernment.

> *"There shall not be found among you any one that maketh his son or his daughter to pass through the fire, or that useth divination, or an observer of times, or an enchanter, or a witch. Or a charmer, or a consulter with familiar spirits, or a wizard, or a necromancer. For all that do these things are an abomination unto the Lord: and because of these abominations the Lord thy God doth drive them out from before thee. Thou shalt be perfect with the Lord thy God. For these nations, which thou shalt possess, hearkened unto observers of times, and unto diviners: but as for thee, the Lord thy God hath not suffered thee so to do" (Deuteronomy 18: 10-14).*

Satan can fake this gift to fool Christians into believing they are receiving instructions from God. So, the Christian must be careful not to be deceived by any counterfeited gift. Only the

Holy Spirit can give the unique ability to understand what the normal human mind cannot ordinarily comprehend.

This gift is given to guide the church away from the many deceptions of the adversary and to take the believer's attention from the spiritual illusions that can distract a Christian's focus from Christ and kingdom realities. It is a gift which authenticity can also be tested by the rule of scripture.

> *"Beloved, believe not every spirit, but try the spirits whether they are of God: because many false prophets are gone out into the world. Hereby know ye the Spirit of God: Every spirit that confesseth that Jesus Christ is come in the flesh is of God: And every spirit that confesseth not that Jesus Christ is come in the flesh is not of God: and this is that spirit of antichrist, whereof ye have heard that it should come; and even now already is it in the world" (1 John 4: 1-3).*

The human mind is limited to what the natural senses can only perceive. And because there are things that exist in the spirit realm which the natural mind cannot perceive, this gift helps the believer to understand when a vision or revelation is from God or the Devil. It acts as a spiritual alarm system to confirm something that is good or warn when something or somewhere is evil. It is like a spiritual identification-system that helps distinguish between true and false prophecies.

> *"But as it is written, Eye hath not seen, nor ear heard, neither have entered into the heart of man, the things which God hath prepared for them that love him. But God hath revealed them unto us by his Spirit: for the Spirit*

searcheth all things, yea, the deep things of God" (1 Corinthians 2: 9-10).

The gift of discernment of spirit is a supernatural ability that separates truth from falsehood, as well as good from evil. A person endowed with this gift will be prompted by the Holy Spirit to perceive what God is showing or displaying for the church. Those who discern by the power of the Holy Spirit usually have a sound mind.

Imagine what the church will be like without the Holy Spirit and his gifts? Christians will be in serious trouble. They will be unable to differentiate between what is right from that which is wrong, or good from evil. In that case there will be no such thing as good moral value. Good will be called evil and evil seen as good.

So, the power of discernment of spirits is not just the mere ability to see spirit beings. Rather, it is a gift of the Holy Spirit upon believers to enable them perceive activities in the spirit realm. And to rightly apply what was shown in the spirit realm on the natural sphere, to the glory of God.

The Bible points out that there are several unclean spirits parading the earth. They include witches, wizards, marine spirits, familiar spirits, spirits of divination, and many other occult spirits. So, it is only by the supernatural gift of discernment that the activities of these foul spirits can be distinguished from the spirits that are from God (Matthew 10:1; Luke 6: 18).

"Beloved, believe not every spirit, but try the spirits whether they are of God: because many false prophets are gone out into the world. Hereby know ye the Spirit of God: Every spirit that confesseth that Jesus Christ is come in the flesh is of God: And every spirit that confesseth

not that Jesus Christ is come in the flesh is not of
God: and this is that spirit of antichrist, whereof
ye have heard that it should come; and even now
already is it in the world" (1 John 4: 1-3).

No child of God should be fooled by lying signs and wonders performed by foul spirits to believe that the manifestations are from God. No one should be gullible to accept the work of Satan as a manifestation from God. Even if a preacher, teacher or prophet works a miracle and claims it is from God, the Christian must be convinced that the miracle is consistent with the teachings of Christ.

A Christian endowed with this wonderful "gift of discerning spirits" will easily identify the false miracles, prophecies and teachings of foul spirits and tell which true message is from God. For the gift is given to perceive what God is showing to the church. And those who discern by the power of the Holy Spirit usually have a sound mind.

It is a wonderful gift that helps expose deception. It enables Christians to flee from the strategies and snares of the adversary before it is too late. It sensitizes the believer ahead of time, motivating him to stand firm on the truth of God and to choose what is the truth irrespective of any satanic seduction.

One sound method of evaluating what has been discerned or validating its source is to consider if the revelation, vision or dream agrees completely with the word of God. A good example is illustrated by the Apostle Paul's encounter with a slave-girl who operated by the spirit of divination in Philippi (Acts 16: 17).

This girl's correct identification of The Apostles Paul and Silas would have deceived the ordinary, powerless Christian. But because Apostles Paul and Silas were filled with the Holy Ghost and operated by the true gift of discernment, they immediately knew what they were dealing with and wasted no time in setting that slave-girl free from the spirit of divination.

Any spiritual experience in the life of a Christian that results in incredible fear without comfort, accusation with no room for remediation, oppression with no hope for redemption, intimidation without divine intervention or ends in a nightmare, should be considered to emanate from the Devil.

The gift of discernment of spirits protects believers from the influence of false teachings. The believer who is content with the teachings of the Holy Spirit will not be deceived by false teachers. These false teachers and their teachings bring divisions in the body of Christ, hinder the gospel and lead believers away from the presence of God.

2). **The power gifts.**

Power gifts constitute a second group of manifestation gifts of the Holy Spirit. They are divine gifts loaded with the supernatural power that enable Christians to accomplish specific purposes in the interest of the Church. And they include:

i). **Gift of faith.**

Faith is an inevitable factor in a believer's relationship with God. It is a vital platform that defines the believer's stand in God. Without faith, no one can please God or fellowship with him. Faith and fellowship with God are connected. Without faith, the Christian's fellowship is in vain.

In the most profound religious sense, faith is the core element or basis of intimacy between God and man. It is the secret code for gaining access into the presence of the almighty God, which is considered as the believer's safest hiding-place.

The beauty of human relationship with God is that it is

divinely initiated. It is a relationship that originates through the silent work of the Holy Spirit. That is why salvation is by faith and not of human works. All that is required from man is the determination to walk with God and consent to work for him.

While there are different forms of faith, one common factor unique to all of them is the unshaken trust in the faithful. This is the basic element of friendship and fellowship between the creator and the creature. Without this dimension of affection, no Christian can please God.

From the Christian religious perspective, faith describes an unashamed loyalty to the Sovereign God. It demonstrates the absolute trust in his word and complete allegiance to his law. It is the un-questionable confidence expressed by a person about God that does not doubt his word or his existence.

It is the believer's, spiritual currency of integrity, the inevitable password between the physical realm and the supernatural sphere, his substance of hope and the key that opens the door for effective divine communication. It is spiritual catalyst for expediting a result-oriented prayer exercise.

"The Lord shall judge the people: judge me, O Lord, according to my righteousness, and according to mine integrity that is in me" (Psalms 7: 8)

Beyond being a vital instrument of spiritual warfare, faith serves as a shield of protection and weapon of defense. The shield of faith, which is "God Most High", as David describes faith in the Psalms, is the best instrument of protection and defense against the attacks by the adversary.

Faithlessness is godlessness. It is evidence of a life bound by sin and that is living without hope. It is the sign of human pride, and an expression of a godless-nature that is independent of the

Supreme deity. A faithless individual is a godless person. He believes in himself and trusts only in his personal abilities.

But Christian faith is different. Generally, this faith represents the action by a believer which causes him to put his hope on God. Thus, the things he expects in the natural sphere are first conceived in the spirit realm. It is this absolute trust in God that causes immaterial things which a believer has prayed for to manifest to him as if they already exist in the natural.

Different expressions of faith are encountered in the Bible, with each of them working according to its respective purpose. Some of these include:

a). **No faith (Deuteronomy 32:20).**

It is difficult to explain the concept of "no faith" without making it seem to contradict other standard definitions of faith. Notwithstanding, "no faith" in the context of scripture is the condition of failing to expend the currency of inherent faith, as though it did not exist. Other expressions of faith include:

b). **Little faith (Matthew 6: 30; 8: 26).**

c). **Believing faith or saving faith (Ephesians 2:8).**

This type of faith is given to all at birth. It is the faith required gain salvation experience.

d). **Gift of faith (I Corinthians 12: 9)**

This kind of faith cannot be replicated or regulated, and it is neither deserved, merited or earned.

e). **Fruit of faith.**

The fruit of faith comes with a believer's continuously growth in the word of God. This growth comes by listening to the word, meditating and acting on what is studied and heard.

f). **Small faith (Matthew 17: 20)**

g). **Great faith (Matthew 8:10)**

h). **Healing faith (Matthew 9:22; 15:28)**

i). **Purifying faith (Acts 15: 9).**

j). **Sanctifying faith (Acts 26: 18)**

k). **Mutual faith (Romans 1: 12)**

l). **Justifying faith (Roman 3:28)**

m). **Weak faith (Romans 4: 19)**

Faith can be weak or strong. It is comparable to a muscle which only grows stronger with application. A weak faith is not capable of accomplishing great works. However, faith that is fed by hearing God's word grows stronger with time. But when faith is starved and unapplied, it begins to shrink as its "nerves and muscles" become weaker by the day until it can no-longer effectively play its role.

No child of God can afford to face the enemy or confront the challenges of life relying on faith that is untested and weak. This will not delight the heart of God or attract spectacular testimonies. That is why crazy faith is sometimes needful. So, no matter the level of your faith, apply it when in need.

n). **Crazy faith (2 Corinthians 5: 13-14).**

This was the power behind the apostle Paul risking his life to please God. From the time he accepted Jesus as his Lord and Savior, he never again lived to please himself. Instead, he spent that life to honor Christ through whose death his old-self was transformed into a new person.

o). **Hearing faith (Romans 10: 17).**

This is the same concept as believing faith. And it is important to note that not all persons operate at the same measure of faith. One person's measure is different from the others. While one believer's expression of faith can move mountains, the next person's application of faith can seal the heavens from rain or call down fire from above. But whichever is your level of faith, apply it.

p). **Measure of faith (Roman 12:3).**

All human creatures have a measure of faith. And while it is important to appreciate your measure of faith with humility, no one should over-estimate the level of faith at which he operates. A person's measure of faith may not immediately begin to move mountains but by applying it regularly, he soon develops the confidence to deal with headaches, stomach pain, and before you know he begins to raise the dead.

q). **Vain faith (1 Corinthians 15: 14).**

r). **Shield of Faith (Ephesians 6: 16).**

This is one great weapon of warfare. Take it always to the battlefield, because life on earth is filled with constant battles.

s). **Sacrifice, or service of faith (Philippians 2:17).**

t). **Work of faith (1 Thessalonians 1: 3).**

ii). **Gift of healing.**

Spiritual healing is said to occur when wellness in the body returns to normal following divine intervention. It represents the restoration of good health through faith-based prayer(s) only. It does not require the involvement of any form of assistance, whether of medical sciences or from psychic sources.

It is the result of supernatural manifestation of the Holy Spirit on a sick person or diseased condition. This can come about following faith-based prayers by the righteous for a believer in Christ who is afflicted in the spirit, soul or body. For while it is possible to be cured of an ailment by the natural man using other processes, only God can cause divine healing. And except God heals the sick, all medical effort will be futile and to no avail.

Truly, there is power in the word of God to heal the sick. And evidences exist that confirm the healing of sicknesses and diseases by the authority in Jesus name, the stripes of Jesus, and the power in Jesus blood. Howbeit, it is by the gift of healing, conferred by the Holy Spirit that this power to heal is released to the community of Christ.

Healing from God in any manner or form is a token of godly mercies and an act of divine graces. This Gift brings into play the revocation of merited judgment on God's children (mercy) and the expression of his underserved compassion (grace) for upon them.

The gift of spiritual healings is the power through which God's children are renewed, refreshed, revived, restored and given new lease of life so that people of faith can continue to serve God in wellness. In some instances, divine healing follows the act of confession of sins, hearty repentance and a turning away from transgressions. Such steps evoke God's forgiveness and clear the way for restoration to take place in the body.

This gift is available for all Christians. Even some Christian medical practitioners who are filled with God's Holy Spirit, are known to operate in the gift of healing. This, however, is not a pre-requisite for receiving this gift, as many unlearned Christians who are filled with the same power, have been used to heal sicknesses and cast out demons.

The glory of God, represented by the manifest presence of the Holy Spirit, brings order wherever there is disorder. It causes God's light to expose and destroy the dark places that accommodate infirmities in a Christian's body. So, while sin or wickedness can make a believer's body vulnerable to diseases and sickness, the Gift of healing is available to reverse the damage done and restore good health.

In addition to the Gift of healing revealing the mercies of God upon a believer's life, it is also an avenue through which the Holy Spirit restores godly peace to souls that are in distress. This is a necessary step to bringing wellness to the human body broken by sickness and disease.

iii). **Working of miracles.**

Working of miracles is one of the spiritual gifts mentioned in Apostle Paul's epistle to the Corinthians. It is the display of God's power over a touch situation. God accomplishes this by suspending natural laws, not the breaking of them, so that supernatural laws can effect a change that is desired in the physical realm.

Through the working of miracles, instantaneous events that are un-conventional are accomplished. Miracles are said to happen when things naturally thought to be impossible, are instantaneously established following divine intervention and the acts of prayer.

The working of miracles represents the surprising, unexplainable, though welcome, extra-ordinary acts of God. They are acts which cannot be repeated by any natural process or replicated by the established scientific principles. They constitute remarkable events of creative order which outcome contradict all known scientific protocols due to their supernatural dimension.

Where a miracle is involved in a situation, all-natural laws and scientific principles are suspended. Thus, it is only by divine intervention that miracles occur. And in all cases, God uses them to bear witness to himself by allowing things that were not originally possible to come into place for the good of man, or society.

However, not every surprising act can be considered a miracle. Only supernatural events in the natural world, which are consistent with God's word and surpass the accomplishment of any human efforts or scientific principles, can be classified as miracles.

While the process of divine healing and the working miracles may look similar, there is a marked difference between the two. A miracle produces an instant result, whereas divine healing almost always, follows a gradual process. And while all miracles can lead to healing, not every divine healing process is said to be miraculous event.

3). **Vocal gifts.**

These are gifts that operate by saying or declaring something. And include:

- i). **Gift of (diverse) tongues.**
- ii). **Gift of Interpretation of tongues.**
- iii). **Gift of Prophecy.**

i). **Gift of tongues.**

The gift of tongues is given by the Holy Spirit to enable communication of spiritually obtained information to the church. This gift enables Christians to speak in languages previously unknown to them and have the message interpreted by the same or a different person. It is also a powerful prayer instrument that opens the door for the manifestation of other spiritual gifts.

No occasion in Christian history illustrates the impact of the Holy Spirit better than the event that occurred on the day of Pentecost. The manifestation of the gift of tongues that day was real evidence of the fulfilment of God's promise which he spoke more than seven hundred years before, through his prophets.

That day marked the general reversal of the disunity of tongues brought upon mankind by the Holy Trinity in the city of Babel. In the arrogance of mankind, the people of Babel sought to "build a city and a tower whose top may reach unto heaven".

This conceited move by mankind to bring attention to human accomplishment, brought the judgment of God upon the people of Babel. God confused the language by which arrogant humanity controlled his perverted his society. For rather than speak words in honor of God who created the heavens and the earth, man began to speak and seek how to contest God's domain. This was the same sin that dethroned Lucifer from the presence of God.

> *"And they said, Go to, let us build us a city and a tower, whose top may reach unto heaven; and let us make us a name, lest we be scattered abroad upon the face of the whole earth."* *(Genesis 11: 4).*

Because of the presumptuous evil by the people of Babel, God confused their common human language, so that no one could understand each other's speech. The city they intended to build was never completed and all the people were dispersed abroad and scattered all over the face of the earth.

But when the day of Pentecost was fully come however, the Holy Spirit released a spiritual language of unity into the body of Christ. This gift enabled the Christ's disciples to speak intelligibly in different kinds of tongues and languages for the purpose of building Christ's church.

This time around, the disciples of Christ spoke in the mother tongues of many devout men and witnesses who had gathered in Jerusalem. And as they spoke in the languages of citizens of different nations under heaven, all who heard them were amazed at the occurrence.

Speech is powerful. And when the words spoken are anointed by the Holy Spirit, they become even more powerful. At Babel, God judged mankind by confusing their common language, but at Pentecost, he blessed his children with a language of unity.

From the beginning of human creation, the Holy Spirit has always existed with the power. But he did not fully manifest to the church until Christ was glorified. Without his manifestation and gifts, the church will be very powerless and inconsequential.

Thus, speaking in other tongues despite what the natural senses perceive, teaches believers to depend on the Holy Spirit in their walk with God and not to rely on their human senses.

It enables believers to savor the sweet experience of visions, revelations and to sometimes fall into trance. Moreover, it is a gift that works well with the gifts of healing, word of knowledge and discernment of spirits.

Speaking in unknown tongues is the vocal expression of words that are usually incomprehensible to the novice or even new Christian convert. It is a supernatural ability that breaks language barriers through the glorious out-pouring of the Holy Spirit (John 7: 37-39).

This gift is a reward by the Holy Spirit that enables intimate fellowship between the supernatural God who dwells in the spirit sphere, and his children in this natural realm. The experience of speaking in other tongues literarily makes a believer speak in harmony with the language of heaven.

The use of this gift must never be abused. It is a unique gift that reveals the deep things from the mind of God. It should not be mixed with natural feelings, but expressed without fear, as the Holy Spirit gives utterance. And those blessed with this gift must endeavor not lose it.

When there is public speaking in tongues, it is expected that interpretation by the speaker or an interpreter should follow. Interpreting what has been spoken is very necessary.

> *"If any man speak in an unknown tongue, let it be by two, or at the most by three, and that by course; and let one interpret. But if there be no interpreter, let him keep silence in the church; and let him speak to himself, and to God" (1 Corinthians 14: 27-28).*

The gift of tongues includes the abilities to pray and sing in other languages. It is a gift that easily connects the believer to God, bring earth before heaven and links the natural to the supernatural. So, its operation is supposed to constitute a huge part of Christian daily and private life-style. But when in public though, it must be used in orderly manner to the benefit of the congregation.

So, when a person is praying or singing in tongues, interpretation of the tongues must work together. Interpretation of tongues must operate harmoniously with the unknown language or take place immediately after. Otherwise, the unlearned in the congregation will be excluded from the worship.

While other gifts enable believers to serve the church, praying and singing in tongues are given to the saints to personally strengthen them in their daily walk with Christ. The spontaneous use of the Gift of tongues by-passes the natural understanding to connect the speaker or interpreter to the supernatural realm.

It is important to note that every manifestation of the Spirit is a sign of God witnessing to the church or through his children to the world. So, the speaking in other tongues and the interpretations should be done in ways that glorify God and edify his church.

Speaking in other Tongues and Interpretation of Tongues, belong to the church era. They are New Testament phenomena and as a result, Christians are expected to operate in more divine manifestations of the Holy Spirit, than did the early believers who lived before the Holy Spirit was fully revealed.

Unfortunately, this is not so, considering that Christians of this electronic generation are products of a perverted society whose church is the social media. As a result, the "church" is filled with morally inept believers and depraved minds whose faith have been damaged by the evil culture of the computer-age.

A church that is choking with iniquity, packed with polluted minds fixed on pornography from Monday to Saturday, only to appear for service on Sunday, will lack power. The Holy Spirit will not flow in an atmosphere overcome by moral deprivation or effectively operate in an environment overcome by disobedience, sexual lust, racial hate, murder, envy, unforgiveness and economic oppression.

From the beginning of creation, God's glory upon his people was always associated with obedience to his righteous commandment. In the Old Testament scriptures, the divine glory of God was generally referred to as the Spirit of God or Spirit of the Lord.

And whenever God's glory departed from a person or nation, it was usually considered to be in repudiation of sin or in response to rebellion against God's word. However, this glory or Spirit of God always returned following confession of the sins and a hearty repentance.

> *"And the Lord spake unto Moses, saying, See, I have called by name Bezaleel the son of Uri, the son of Hur, of the tribe of Judah: And I have filled him with the spirit of God, in wisdom, and in understanding, and in knowledge, and in all manner of workmanship, To devise cunning works, to work in gold, and in silver, and in brass" (Exodus 31:1-4).*

God's word reminds the child of faith that his gifts and anointing work together. However, anointing by the Holy Spirit and impartation with his gifts should not negate a believer's need to obey divine statutes. Obedience to God's word must precede the working of the anointing.

The modern church is operating at the lowest level of spiritual power because most Pastors have lost their focus on Christ and the Holy Spirit. That is why pride, disobedience, lust and deceit sit comfortably unchallenged on many church pews. These negative influences have become common occurrences because solid Christian values have been compromised.

The early disciples were different. They had real concern for perishing souls, deep fear of God, zeal for intimate fellowship with him and engaged in respectful relationship with Christ. They lived in eager expectation of the promise of the Father, were hungry for the Holy Spirit and his gifts, and followed God's word to the letter.

They clearly understood that there was incredible power of divine gifts given by the Father, dispensed by the Son, and manifested via the work of the Holy Spirit who dwells in the believer. As a result, they zealously sought after, eagerly desired, and earnestly coveted these gifts.

The same gifts are still available to the modern Christian. But the child of God who desires to operate at any significant level in the flow of divine power and gifts, must persistently ask, seek, and knock on the door of heaven, with fear and humility, until their request is honored.

ii). **Interpretation of tongues.**

The ability to interpret unknown tongues is a supernatural gift. This gift is given by the Holy Ghost to make what is spoken in "unknown tongues", to become beneficial to the church. It is a New Testament gift to the church and is listed in the twelfth chapter of apostle Paul's first epistle to the Corinthians.

This gift correctly explains in a common or natural language, what is spoken in spiritual parlance. This is not a skill that follows the pattern of any linguistic translation and so, cannot be taught, mimicked or learned. And because it is a gift from God, the process of its translation is guided by the Holy Spirit to ensure that the original content of the message is intact.

Interpretation of tongues is a gift that helps the church understand divine messages originally spoken in incomprehensible tongue. Without interpretation, the message to the church would be meaningless. This can have dangerous consequences.

The "Gift of interpretation of tongues" represents a type of prophecy, except that prophecies are not veiled. Prophecies are usually open messages and are direct. But by interpreting tongues, whatever is concealed in a message that is given to the Church is finally unsealed.

The process of interpreting tongues must not engage in embellishment of the message and must not attempt to subtract, diminish or devalue what was spoken in other tongues. So, when a person is praying or singing publicly in tongues, there must be a follow-up by interpretation. Interpretation of tongues must operate harmoniously with the unknown language or take place immediately after. This is to ensure that everyone in the congregation is carried along.

In this manner, the church is edified, the unlearned in the congregation understand what has been communicated and God is glorified.

iii). **Prophecy**

One other significant gift of the Holy Spirit to the church is the gift of Prophecy. It is a vocal gift that represents a unique form of communicating privileged information from God through a believer, specifically to the body of Christ or even to a heathen people or leader.

The "Gift of prophecy" is very useful tool, not only in time of worship, but always in the life of the Christian who is thus blessed. It is described as a vocal gift because of the distinctive manner it is used for communicating privileged information specifically to Christians and generally to all humanity.

Prophesy is one of the numerous ways through which God relates to his creation. The Gift to prophesy therefore enables a person to hear from God and succinctly deliver the message received from him without variations to another Christian, group of persons, a nation or to the church. It can be messages received on a one-time basis or repeatedly as God desires.

It denotes the inspired utterance or prediction of events that are yet to happen, as given by the Spirit of God through his children. However, not all persons who prophesy are designated as Prophets. God makes this choice and can speak through any person or thing.

Thus, the concept of prophecy must not be confused with the divine calling into the consecrated office of the Prophet. Prophets are God's chosen servants. They are intermediaries appointed by God to proclaim divine secrets and teach the knowledge of God's will to man.

The Holy Spirit confers this special ability to prophesy on anyone of his choice, irrespective of their age, gender or race. Primarily, it works through people that interact with the Holy Spirit and who are willing to serve the church and humanity at large, without fear. But God can use anyone or thing as desires.

> *"For the prophecy came not in the old time by the will of man: but holy men of God spake as they were moved by the Holy Spirit" (2 Peter 1: 21).*

So, it must be understood that being used in any form or manner to prophesy, does not confer the title of prophet on the instrument that was used. Because, while anybody or thing can be used to prophesy, not all such vessels are called to be prophets.

No one gets to operate in this gift for any special merit, quality, or human accomplishment. God once used an animal to speak to a rebellious seer called Balaam, the son of Beor, in the matter of Balak and the children of Israel.

> *"And the LORD opened the mouth of the ass, and she said unto Balaam, what have I done unto thee that thou hast smitten me these three times" (Numbers 22: 28).*

God's message is never confusing. It is usually very clear and concise, even when it sounds unreasonable. The messenger of God is just a vessel and is not accountable for the outcome of the message. So, anyone prophesying is supposed to give the message exactly as it has been received from God. It is dangerous practice for a person to add anything to or delete any part of the message while rendering God's message.

PRAYER POINTS.

1). Holy Spirit, fill me with power to understand spiritual things, in Jesus name.

2). Holy Spirit, fill me with the spirit of excellent knowledge, in Jesus name.

3). I receive divine wisdom to excel above all others, in Jesus name.

4). O Lord, open my eyes to see wonderful things of your kingdom, in Jesus name.

5). Holy Spirit, let me hear your sweet, soft voice, in Jesus name.

6). I shall not succumb to counterfeiting spirits, in Jesus name.

7). I refuse to dabble into any form of spiritism, in Jesus name.

8). Bread of heaven, feed me with supernatural knowledge, in Jesus name.

9). I flee from every seduction of occult cosmic attraction, in Jesus name.

10). Holy Spirit, empower me with the faith that subdues fear, in Jesus name.

11). By the authority of the Holy Spirit, I employ my faith to part waters, in Jesus name.

12). Faithful God, fulfill your promises in every area of my life, in Jesus name.

13). I receive the "crazy faith" that will move mountains, in Jesus name.

14). Miracle working God, do a special thing in my life, in Jesus name.

CHAPTER

TEN

Fruit of the Holy Spirit

It is amazing that all divine gifts and fruit, even when they are associated with God the Father or God the Son, are somehow linked by title to the Holy Spirit. This is because, the Holy Spirit is the person of the divine Trinity presently indwelling all believers. He is God's contact point with the Christian and Christ's witness to his church.

Unfortunately, there is an obvious attempt by the enemy of the human soul to hinder the manifestation of God's gifts or the bearing of Chris-like fruits by the church. The way he does this is by flaunting a seductive culture of fashion, speech, music and perverse life-style that are irresistible to the human eyes but destroy the soul.

And in an already broken world where human pride, institutionalized hate, sexual perversion, economic oppression and demonic wickedness are in serious contention with the ways of God, the desire godly sacrificial living is not expected to be one of man's greatest strengths. In that circumstance, any attempt to maintain purity of heart or bear Christ-like fruit will immediately meet with persecution from even the most unexpected quarters of life.

In this society, as in most advanced places in the world, bearing Christlike fruit is the least item on many people's agenda, including even Christians. From the moment of waking up in the morning to the time of retiring to bed, life is literarily pursued by obscenities, possessed by vanities and embroiled in odious perversions. And when on a daily basis, the human mind is brought under this constant barrage of moral and spiritual abuses, bearing fruit becomes a tough job.

The Devil is currently responsible for this world system. And he is determined through his tightly operated evil network in the fashion, financial system, electronic and print media to invalidate the redemptive work of Christ and obstruct the work of the Holy Spirit.

He is aware that souls arrested by poverty and polluted by an atmosphere of sin will be morally depraved, emotionally destabilized, easily angered, wrathful at the slightest or no provocation, bitter, lawless in the spirit, and full of hatred. This explains the orgy of senseless murder, rape, and terrorism thriving unchecked, all over the world. Which is the reason the world needs the Holy Spirit today more than ever before.

For after a person receives Christ as his personal Lord and Savior, the bondage of the law that produced evil fruits in that life is completely broken. A new heart is revealed that gradually weans itself of the appetite to do evil, express hate and hold unnecessary grudge against others. It is then that a new spirit and a new man is born.

As descendants of the fallen Adam, every human creature needs this new heart and a burning desire to reconnect with the heavenly Father. And the only way this can be achieved is through the work of the Holy Spirit. That is the path of a reprobate soul to Christ before he can bear fruit that will delight the heart of God.

Until a person is converted and begins to operate in the gifts of his calling, that person cannot be useful in the kingdom of God. Such a person remains like fallow ground or barren tree. But a converted, fruit-bearing Christian pleases God and is rewarded with favors when he prays.

*"Ye have not chosen me, but I have chosen you,
and ordained you, that ye should go and bring
forth fruit, and that your fruit should remain:
that whatsoever ye shall ask of the Father in my
name, he may give it you" (John 15: 16).*

A fruit-bearing Christian is eager to identify with Christ's regenerating virtues and character. He is ever ready to embrace the ideals that defined Christ's glorious nature. He is bold, fearless, firmly established in the service of the kingdom and is not ashamed of the indelible marks of persecution on his body.

These are the characters that define those Christians who desire to be transformed into flourishing branches of the spiritual vine. It is such branches that become light in a dark and perishing world. God is pleased to use them and never fails to reward their labor of love.

God desires that all Christians bear useful fruit. The Christlike fruit produced by the believer will influence the lives of others in the church and society for good. But this can only be accomplished in souls completely surrendered to Christ and totally transformed by the Holy Spirit.

Jesus calls all believers to a fruit-bearing enterprise. And those who accept this invitation are entrusted with the power to influence the world for his kingdom. Bearing useful and lasting fruit have their benefits which include receiving whatever is asked from the Father, in the name of Jesus.

The fruit of the Spirit is key to operating with God. And any one of the under-listed fruit or a combination of them will undoubtedly open the flood-gate of answered prayers to the believer who faithfully, and consistently asks, seeks, or knocks at the door of heaven, in prayer.

There are nine major spiritual fruit that characterize a Christian that is completely surrendered to Christ. These include:

1). **The fruit of Love.**

There are several classifications of the human emotion described as love. Seven major types of this expression can be identified between the spiritual and carnal forms. These include:

i). **Philia love.**

Philia love describes a form of natural emotion that characterizes human affection. This feeling is a sign of deep friendship that is instinctive to man. It is a natural kind of feeling that exists between friends and is common among siblings. The expression of philia emotion is generally impulsive.

It is also described as "friendly" or "brotherly love" and is a highly valued type of feeling as it is seen as deep affection between two equals. It is the type of feeling that is not defined by physical attraction but is expressed among friends who have come a long way or endured hard-time together.

ii). **Eros kind of love.**

This emotion is specifically associated with sexual passion. It is the affectionate feeling behind romantic love affairs. This is the "consuming", emotional fire that leads to consensual sex. It has less value than philia love.

iii). **The "Ludus" love.**

Ludus is a feeling that describes the superficial, uncommitted, flirtatious affection of one person for another. Although it is casual, it is seductive and can be miss-interpreted by any of the parties involved in the relationship to mean something serious. It can be described as playful or unserious love.

It is the general type of emotion expressed between most young people in a first relationships. Unfortunately, many hearts get crushed because the devil takes advantage of the wrong notions formed in this weak bonding to lead people astray.

iv). Pragma type of love.

This kind of affection is based more on personal qualities, shared goals, and common interests, rather than the desire for sex (Eros). It describes the aged and matured affection formed over time in a relationship. It is the product of efforts by the parties involved and is built through patience, tolerance and compromise.

But a Christian has to be careful, especially if the bonding goals shared in a "Pragma" relationship are not established by the Holy Spirit.

v). Storge.

This is another dimension of the "philia" kind of love. It describes the natural fondness between parents and their children. Often described as familial love, it is an intimate affection existing especially between parents and their younger children.

It also describes the affection shared among childhood friends which is carried over to adult life.

vi). Philautia.

Philautia is the feeling that describes the love for self. This is not the self-love that leads to superiority complex over others, pride, self-obsession or vanity. It is not based on physical beauty, fame or fortune but grows out of the understanding that loving others begins with loving one-self. No one can give what he does not have.

vii). **Agape love.**

Every living being has an intrinsic ability to exhibit any of the passionate emotions described above. But there is a form of intimacy that goes beyond all carnal emotions. This is because it is the product of selfless sacrifice closest only to Christ's type of selfless and unconditional love.

This is known as "Agape Love". Agape love describes spiritual love. It is God's kind of love. It is a deep affection that overflows with compassion for others and the selfless desire to serve their needs in response to the work of the Holy Spirit. This kind of love is boundless and transcends every human feeling.

Agape love depicts the very essence of God's nature. The closest illustration of this character is depicted by God's gift to the world. For "God so loved the world that he gave his only Son" (John 3: 16). It is love driven by the passion for sacrificial living, unselfish concern for others, limitless generosity and sincere kindness.

It is not sentimental or mere emotional affection, but pure love that is devoid of any expectations. It is loving others, regardless of their human flaws, race, antecedents, religious beliefs or sociocultural orientations. This is the Christ's kind of love. And man can only be like Christ by loving like he did.

Love is the hallmark of the Christian faith. God's love is divine, yet he was willing to sacrifice his divinity in heaven and lower himself into the world that he may express his very nature to his children. God's message of love is therefore one of compassion, kindness, humility and selfless-service.

Thus, as images of God, Christians are expected to reflect

his divine characters by selflessly caring, humbly serving, and sacrificially pouring out their lives for others. This is the fruit-bearing act that appeals to God and delights his spirit. And because it is modelled after Christ's example, it opens the gateway into his presence through the Holy Spirit.

The Agape kind of love, which fruit is produced through the agency of the Holy Spirit is patient, kind, does not envy or boast, is not proud, not rude and is not self-seeking. It is not easily offended, holds no malice, does not delight in evil and keeps no record of grudges.

Agape love rejoices in truth, does not hate, is protective of other Christians and neighbors, is full of trust and does not betray others. It mourns with those that mourn, celebrates with those that celebrate, rejoices at the success of others, lives in hope, perseveres and never disappoints.

A Christian that is not baptized by the Holy Spirit will only operate at the illusory level of this kind of love. It is only as the influence of the Holy Spirit comes alive in a believer that he can replicate these self-less characters of Christ.

> *"So when they had dined, Jesus saith to Simon Peter, Simon, son of Jonas, lovest thou me more than these? He saith unto him, Yea, Lord; thou knowest that I love thee. He saith unto him, Feed my lambs. He saith to him again the second time, Simon, son of Jonas, lovest thou me? He saith unto him, Yea, Lord; thou knowest that I love thee. He saith unto him, Feed my sheep" (John 21: 15-16).*

This is the kind of fruit that God desires every Christian to reproduce. It is not only self-less but renders sacrificial service to the body of Christ. And even though it may seem impossible in a morally broken world, it is very possible and practicable with the help of the Holy Spirit.

2). Fruit of Joy.

Another fruit, which God desires that Christians produce, is the fruit of joy. Happiness and gladness are a two very wonderful feelings to experience. But the joy of the Lord is beyond these emotions. Joy of the Holy Ghost is eternal and is not controlled by the environment or human circumstances.

The virtue of joy was a very central in the daily life and ministry of Christ on earth. And Christians who desire to be like Christ are persuaded to bear this satisfying fruit. Its unique attribute enables Christians to function at levels of uninterrupted praise. This fruit explains why a child of God will maintain a good countenance even in the face of a deep trial.

Like other spiritual fruit such as love, faithfulness, gentleness and patience, the character of joy is a feeling that does not fluctuate with circumstances. To experience and express it, a believer must model himself after the life of Christ and share in his passion to save souls.

All those who encountered Christ, experienced some degree of this joy. Ordinarily hearing about Jesus' birth evoked this kind of joy in the lives of gentile shepherds. Also, people who heard Jesus minister the gospel, experienced great joy. And Jesus' early disciples were filled with this joy, just as the over-flow of this virtue in Jesus early disciples was responsible for their zeal in ministry.

> *"And the people with one accord gave heed unto those things which Philip spake, hearing and seeing the miracles which he did. For unclean spirits, crying with loud voice, came out of*

many that were possessed with them: and many taken with palsies, and that were lame, were healed. And there was great joy in that city" *(Acts 8: 6-8).*

"And the seventy returned again with joy, saying, Lord, even the devils are subject unto us through thy name" (Luke 10: 17-19).

The fruit of joy will cause a believer to chase after God's vision for his kingdom with Christ-like passion. It is what makes faithful Christians to become a world-changer for God's kingdom.

In the journey of life, a Christian will be confronted with many persecutions, trials and frustrations. When these trials do not come from family members or close associates, they will come through friends turned adversaries. It is this fruit that will enable the persecuted to cope when such challenges arise.

Only Christians in fellowship with Christ and who spend purposeful time with the Holy Spirit can experience the glorious power and blissful out-pouring of this joy of the Lord. Those filled with this kind of joy of are not troubled by the challenges of life.

"Thou wilt show me the path of life: in thy presence is the fulness of joy; at thy right hand are pleasures for evermore "(Psalms 16: 11).

The power to bear this fruit begins the moment a child of God is baptized in the Holy Ghost. But three important things to understand about the fruit of joy are,

i). This joy must not be confused with happiness, which is contentment based on circumstances of life. For while happiness is the momentary display of pleasure, this joy is an enduring feeling that is not affected by adverse conditions.

ii). Authentic joy therefore, is a feeling of complete satisfaction that is consistent through all seasons of life. It is a state of delight that comes from knowing God.

iii). Joy is the lasting pleasure or satisfaction that develops with being in a right relationship with God.

The joy of the Lord is a fruit of the spirit that is produced in believers. It grows out of the spiritual truth that God is in control of every situation in life and is established on the understanding that only godly-comfort overcomes all misery. It reveals the willful character of a Christian whose faith is firm, irrespective of his condition of life. This Joy of the Lord surpasses all happiness that material wealth, fame, luxury or worldly security can provide.

A believer in whose heart the Holy Spirit reigns can be sure to experience the lasting joy of God whether in good times or in challenging situations. Especially if such a Christian consciously determines to cling to God, no matter what challenges he is experiencing.

> *"Glory and honour are in his presence; strength and gladness are in his place"* (1 Chronicles 16: 27).

> *"Thou wilt shew me the path of life: in thy presence is fulness of joy; at thy right hand there are pleasures for evermore" (Psalms 16: 11).*

The joy of the Lord is of in-estimable value. Its power releases divine strength and transforms the believer's state of mourning into exhilarating season of great celebration. It is God's gift through which he rewards his faithful children. This joy makes a believer to rejoice even in the face of trouble.

"Then he said unto them, Go your way, eat the fat, and drink the sweet, and send portions unto them for whom nothing is prepared: for this day is holy unto our Lord: neither be ye sorry; for the joy of the Lord is your strength" *(Nehemiah 8: 10).*

"Thou hast turned for me my mourning into dancing: thou hast put off my sackcloth, and girded me with gladness" (Psalms 30: 11).

The fruit of Joy is evidence of a spirit-led life. And a Christian who walks with the Lord, and works for him, is enabled by the Holy Spirit to enjoy a fulfilled life, regardless of the circumstances around him.

This invaluable fruit of the spirit is for those people through whose brokenness the world can see the bright light of God's glory. It is like a spiritual magnet that can make unbelievers to desire the graces of Christ's spiritual riches. It is Christ, through the Holy Spirit that endows the Christian with the ability to bear this fruit.

3). **Fruit of Peace.**

The world is desperate for peace, especially as weapons that can easily destroy the entire universe at the soft-press of a nuclear button are now readily available. We all need peace, whether in the family, at the work place, at school, in the public, leisure or sports arena. Unfortunately, the search for enduring peace is focused at the wrong places.

So, the world we live in and certainly human hearts will remain unsafe until spiritual and political world leaders begin to look in the right place. And where else can that be but in the reliable word of God. That is the only trusted place where enduring peace dwells. Until man returns to this secure place, lasting peace will remain a mirage or a fantasy.

The wealth of the nations, and all their technological attainments can only lead to pride, wars and more wars. No nation will stop researching for new arsenal as each nation will try to prove why her own military might is more potent and more technologically advanced than the others.

National wealth and human success cannot provide this peace. It cannot be found through population growth, by amassing stealth weapons for warfare, and definitely not at the conference tables chaired by politically advanced nations. It can only be found in God before whom disorder cannot exist. So, it is only with the return of humanity to God that the nations can find this peace.

One of God's numerous titles is: Jehovah Shalom. This literarily translated means "The Lord is Peace". This was the title by which God revealed himself to Gideon in a very dark time in Israel's history. God always manifests to his children in time of confusion to bring order in their lives even when they do not deserve it.

> *"Then Gideon built an altar there unto the Lord, and called it Jehovah Shalom: unto this day it is yet in Ophrah of the Abiezrites" (Judges 6: 24).*

Shalom is a Hebrew word that describes the state of peace. Generally, peace implies the condition of calm. But in Hebrew language, the word shalom has a deeper meaning than just the absence of conflict or hostility. More that these, it refers to a person's total wellbeing, soundness of mind, success and general completeness.

In a wider sense, it is a symbol of both internal and external calmness that represents total harmony and concord. It is freedom from disturbance, disagreement, or disorder. And it represents life in an utmost, undisturbed condition of mind.

Before time, God was mindful of a time when sin in a broken world will not permit a stable state of the human-mind. He foreknew that Christians of that age will face challenges that will distort natural order. And when that time came, he sent his Son, Jesus Christ (the Prince of Peace), to reveal this peace to the world, for the sake of the church.

> *"For unto us a child is born, unto us a son is given: and the government shall be upon his shoulder: and his name shall be called Wonderful, Counsellor, The mighty God, The everlasting Father, The Prince of Peace"* *(Isaiah 9: 6).*

God is sensitive to the believer's basic human needs for survival. And because a significant portion of this need is peace, he provided it through his Son, Jesus Christ. It is God's desire not only to ensure that his righteous children experience daily peace, but that they extend it to others by replicating it in their church and world.

> *"For I know the thoughts that I think toward you, saith the Lord, thoughts of peace, and not of evil, to give you an expected end"* *(Jeremiah 29: 11).*

Sin thrives in disorder and generates wickedness, hatred and bitterness. Neither of these encourage godly peace. So, it is only through those lives filled with the Holy Spirit that God can reveal his Christ-like peace to the church. Jesus was an embodiment of this peace. He not only modelled this invaluable virtue but promised it to give it to his disciples. That is why God expects the believer in Christ to regularly bear the fruit of peace.

> *"Peace I leave with you, my peace I give unto you: not as the world giveth, give I unto you. Let not your heart be troubled, neither let it be afraid" (John 14: 27).*

4). **Fruit of Longsuffering.**

Longsuffering is another word for patience. It is the capacity to tolerate delay, permit suffering, and condone hardship while serving God and the church, without getting angry or losing faith. This is a character that is developed through spiritual growth in the word of God.

It is the hallmark of faithful Christians and all people of faith who in the face of misfortune, provocation, or other difficult situations remain calm, and unruffled through the time of discomfort. It is showing patient-endurance in-spite of pain, especially from troubles caused by others. Christ exhibited this character during his incarnation despite being the Son of God.

The Christian who desires to walk in the foot-steps of Christ must possess this virtue. Christ showed respect and self-control in his dealings with the religious leaders of his day. He refused to be un-necessarily provoked and patiently interacted with folks of all works of life without berating them, insulting their ego or demeaning their weak human abilities.

In the same manner, Christ expects his Holy Spirit filled disciples to do the same. To treat others with the godly respect rather than get easily irritated, bored or refuse to understand other people's situations. A long-suffering Christian is full of compassion for the hurting, forebears with the weak, easily forgives, expresses empathy, is honest to his own hurt and goes out of his way to show kindness to others all the time.

"But thou, O Lord, art a God full of compassion, and gracious, long suffering, and plenteous in mercy and truth" (Psalms 85: 15).

Longsuffering does not however disarm the faithful believer from his legitimate right to react to significant unjust conditions. In such circumstances, raising honest objections does not violate the concept. But constitutes a righteous exception to the rule.

The long-suffering nature of God is the only reason this cruel, wicked and oppressive world-system has not been destroyed. So, while Christians wait for the return of Christ for his church, there must be a deliberate effort to patiently reach out to the helpless, the poor and perishing souls, so that they can be saved for Christ.

5). **Fruit of Gentleness.**

In this morally devasted world, where human survival depends on the muscles of the fittest, victory in all areas of life has become a thing that only bullies enjoy. And when patience and humility have little attraction to humanity, gentleness becomes a character that many will not covet.

But because Christians are not supposed to be like the people of the world, the significant identity that singles out any true child of God in the society, is this attitude of gentleness. This character of moderation was consistent with Christ for which reason the multitude admired and flocked to him. He was always cautious of other people's feelings, calm in dealing with contrary views and avoided violence.

In fact, many bible illustrations point to the meek character of our Lord Jesus, depicting him as a person with unusual humility and of broken spirit. This explains why he is often spoken of figuratively, as a lamb. The demeanor of a lamb is unimaginably gentle.

Sadly, the godly virtue of gentleness has been misinterpreted in our broken world to mean weakness, spinelessness, or being feeble, which is not so. Rather, gentleness represents the attitude of being considerate, and of un-assuming disposition. It is the quality of being peaceable, and mild.

> *"But we were gentle among you, even as a nurse*
> *cherisheth her children" (1 Thessalonians 2: 7)*

Jesus described himself as meek. And concerning Moses, God said he was the meekest person that ever lived on earth. A meek or gentle person is one whose spirit is broken. He is never proud, conceited or arrogant. Despite his strength, knowledge or accomplishments, a person of gentle character always brings himself under control.

Thus, gentleness expressed in any form by a believer, is indicative of a life completely surrendered to Jesus and totally filled in the inner-man by the power of Holy Spirit. Gentle persons are calm and do not un-necessarily boast or display their abilities.

> *"He was oppressed, and he was afflicted, yet*
> *he opened not his mouth: he is brought as a*
> *lamb to the slaughter, and as a sheep before her*
> *shearers is dumb, so he openeth not his mouth"*
> *(Isaiah 53: 7).*

> *"But I was like a lamb or an ox that is brought*
> *to the slaughter; and I knew not that they*
> *had devised devices against me, saying, Let*
> *us destroy the tree with the fruit thereof, and*

let us cut him off from the land of the living,
that his name may be no more remembered."
(Jeremiah 11: 19).

In the spiritual community as well as in the secular world, the gentle approach to issues always subdues difficult circumstances. Abigail's story in the Bible helps to illustrate how by her soft persuasion, she turned the mind of David from destroying Nabal (her first husband) and her entire household (Proverbs 25: 15). A gentle spirit is eagerly submissive to divine command because it is through the gentle whisper of the Holy Spirit that God reveals himself.

"A soft answer turneth away wrath: but
grievous words stir up anger" (Proverbs 15: 1).

Through gentle acts, violence is defeated, and unrighteous anger, pride, arrogance and harshness brought under control. This is a virtue associated with Christians that are rich in humility and overflow with tender loving-warmth and humility. A gentle person is tame but not timid, mild but not mindless, of genteel behavior, tender and never vulgar. He is also affable, and courteous.

Such Christians have pleasant temper, are sweet in nature, tender in attitude, and are very easy to be appeased when offended. They are calm towards others, do not bear grudges to their hurt, and are never bitter towards people, particularly those perceived to be inferior to them in any consideration.

For this reason, Christians are admonished to submit to this affable dimension of the Holy Spirit. Through his un-assuming nature, a Christian can reach the world for Christ with the same attitude that Jesus influenced perishing souls for his heavenly Father.

6). Fruit of Goodness.

It is very easy to identify a person of good character in any gathering. And just as a person of vicious nature is easily identifiable in the society, an individual with good virtues cannot be hidden. In a depraved age like ours, goodness cannot be hidden as it is a morally upright virtue that easily reveals itself. It is virtuous quality that defines a Christian in good standing with the word of God.

> *"Either make the tree good, and his fruit good; or else make the tree corrupt, and his fruit corrupt: for the tree is known by his fruit. O generation of vipers, how can ye, being evil, speak good things? for out of the abundance of the heart the mouth speaketh. A good man out of the good treasure of the heart bringeth forth good things: and an evil man out of the evil treasure bringeth forth evil things. (Matthew 12: 33-35).*

Goodness is character mostly associated with the good things of God. It reveals itself through God's divine love, kindness, compassion, and other praise-worthy virtues of the Divine Trinity. It involves the untiring attitude to do good works and is characterized by great moral rectitude, integrity, honesty, and other worthy conducts that worldly people find difficult to imbibe.

A good person is identified by these virtues because of the influence of the Holy Spirit upon him. Such people are known for their insatiable desire for justice, selfless service in the kingdom of God, open-mindedness that gladly highlights the goodness in others, desire for equity, holiness, purity and their fear of God.

Goodness flows from a heart indwelt by the Holy Spirit. It is an attitude that causes the believer to help the helpless and provide hope for the hopeless and the human dregs in our society. This fruit makes people consciously choose to do good and condemn evil.

The fruit of goodness causes people to deliberately live in uprightness, behave decently towards others and stay away from things that are evil. God's goodness is the foundation of scripture. It is revealed in the books of the law, sung in the Psalms, spoken of by the prophets, praised in biblical historicity, is affirmed in the gospels, and generally echoed in the epistles.

"Either make the tree good, and his fruit good; or else make the tree corrupt, and his fruit corrupt: for the tree is known by his fruit. O generation of vipers, how can ye, being evil, speak good things? for out of the abundance of the heart the mouth speaketh. A good man out of the good treasure of the heart bringeth forth good things: and an evil man out of the evil treasure bringeth forth evil things" (Matthew 12: 33-35).

Across the bible, several scriptures describe the net-effect of God's goodness, specifically towards his Children. Christian's are therefore expected to model their lives after this character. And because this character comes from God, its standard might seem un-attainable like the others. But with the Holy Spirit, it is not an impossible fruit to bear. God generally rewards people of good character but condemns those or evil moral behavior

"Woe unto them that call evil good, and good evil; that put darkness for light, and light for

*darkness; that put bitter for sweet, and sweet
for bitter!" (Isaiah 5: 20).*

God is good, and desires that his children adopt his nature.
By this blue-print, all mankind can experience him as he reveals
his wonderful works to the church and the world. Thus, this God
inspired goodness is given so that through its expression, others
can be blessed in a world grossly influenced by the devil where
truth is hard to find and injustice reigns supreme.

7). **Fruit of Faithfulness.**

Faithfulness refers to fidelity. It is a character specifically
ascribed to devotion and describes a person's sense of loyalty,
allegiance or commitment. It is a divine virtue that is usually
linked to God's unchangeable nature and his un-wavering
attributes.

In a wider spiritual sense, faithfulness denotes God's constancy
in relation to his dealings with his children. He is faithful in his
gracious promises in his Word and firm in the eternal covenants
to fulfill them. He is worthy of trust and does not waver, hesitate
or renege in the words that he has spoken. They stand forever.

*"The grass withereth, the flower fadeth: but
the word of our God shall stand for ever"
(Isaiah 40: 8).*

Faithfulness of God denotes firmness, especially in relation
to God's unfailing promises. It is the greatest act of relationship
between the creator and his creatures. God's faithfulness also
describes his character of sincerity which endures to all generations.

"For the Lord is good; his mercy is everlasting; and his truth endureth to all generations" (Psalms 100: 5).

In the Christian form of sacred worship, un-wavering trust is rightly considered the basic element of faith. It is the primary evidence of a Christian's loyalty to God and a fruit of the Spirit that shows that a believer's confidence in Christ is real.

In God's faithfulness towards his children, he forgives the sins of the penitent, loves humanity, steadfastly protects his children against evil and abundantly provides for those who diligently seek him.

But because, faithfulness is not a character that is easily associated with man in his fallen state, God uses Holy Spirit filled Christians who are committed to his kingdom and who uphold the integrity of his word, to sustain the church.

And given the nature of this defiled world, it is difficult to find honest people with trustworthy character who are committed to the unwavering terms of a covenant relationship with God. For this reason, God is looking to raise loyal branches of the vine that will bear the fruit of faithfulness. He is looking for Christians whose unshaken trust can withstand the challenges of this world.

8). Fruit of Kindness.

The Christian must, without fail, let his light shine in a dark world through a life of kindness. He must let his gift be revealed to the world in the way his life affects his society. It was God's kindness to mankind that led him to surrender Christ to die on the cross. By his kindness, he gave his only Son to suffer and die so that all who believe could enjoy eternal life.

Since God never withheld his kindness to undeserving humanity, those who have received such love ought to extend it to others. However, it is not by one flash of kindness that a Christian is counted as being fruitful in the spirit. But through repeated acts compassion, a believer can indeed change a person, a community, his church and the world for Christ.

Kindness is a virtue that flows from God, and the believer with a kind attitude delights the heart of God. Christians that overflow in the character of godly kindness are figuratively described as possessing large hearts. And God always rewards their labor of love.

Honest kindness includes a variety of sympathetic actions shown to relatives, friends, slaves, strangers and even foes. This virtue knows no bounds as it involves the extension of acts of benevolence to others irrespective of their religious beliefs, race, gender or age.

Kindness is the dispensation of selfless generosity and affectionate love towards others. It represents the care for the needy and concern for the helpless, particularly to people of lower means who would not be able to reciprocate the favors shown them.

This virtue involves a habitual outpouring of gracious deeds, a regular inclination to do good always, as well as possessing goodwill for others. Kindness is not just the wish to do good, but actual deed of helping the helpless at all times. Added to giving useful time, talent, and treasure, other meaningful acts of kindness include forgiving others, giving aid towards the aged and helpless, assisting the homeless, the handicapped and opening doors of opportunities to others.

It can involve caring for the needy, helping the helpless, and those of lower means. It is being considerate in the most selfless and sacrificial manner, engaging in habitual outpouring of gracious deeds, being regularly inclined to doing good and possessing goodwill for others.

Kindness is never really an easy virtue to live by since many acts of kindness have been exploited in the past and kind persons rewarded evil for their good. But because God is the source of kindness, every selfless act of generosity has its reward from him. So, God expects Christians to bear the fruit of kindness without fail.

9). Fruit of Temperance

This virtue manifests in the form of self-restraint. It represents a habitual conduct of moderation and typifies the quality of sobriety in an individual. It represents the attitude of calmness even in the midst of confusion.

Temperance is another word for moderation. In a more general sense, it suggests the habit of regulating natural desires, limiting moral cravings and controlling bad instinctive behaviors. It is in the good nature of a Christian to be able to apply restraint, be in control or have mastery over his desires and passions.

Although the fruit of temperance is a gift received from Christ at the time of salvation, it grows out of a disciplined life. But the manifestation of this virtue becomes more evident by the daily work of the indwelling Spirit of God in the life of that believer.

A Christian ruled by a temperate spirit is not violent, brutal or aggressive in behavior. He does not bully others or threaten people's lives. He is always in control of every situation in his life including his appetite, sexual drive, urge for to abuse drugs, use tobacco or consume alcohol.

Temperance is a fruit every Christian should determine to bear. And once produced, this fruit must not be neglected but determinedly improved upon as it can enable that Christian to control his thoughts, tongue, temper, lusts, hunger and thirsts.

It is not in the power of any person to control their habits.

This is where an attitude of complete surrender to the Holy Spirit plays the very important role. It is a life yielded to Christ that is subject to the will of God. Carnal restraints will only lead to moderations whose limits are easily abused. But in a life resigned to Christ and filled with the Holy Spirit, the fear of God helps build a spiritual wall of discipline that cannot be cracked by temptation or either pulled down or scaled by the Devil.

Such Christians are the believers that God can trust with his power for signs, miracles and wonders. He is waiting for them, because it is through these good-natured people that he can transform the world.

The fruit of the Spirit represent major character traits of Christ that can be produced in a Christian by the work of the Holy Spirit. They are produced in lives completely given up to Jesus.

Jesus is the true vine and the believers are the branches. In the Bible, the Lord Jesus encouraged all Christians to abide in him. It is by abiding in him that any believer can bring forth fruit for the kingdom of God. And the Holy Spirit is ever ready to make this come true.

PRAYER POINTS

1). Concerning kingdom matters, I shall bear useful fruit, in Jesus name.

2). My fruit in Christ shall glorify the name of God, in Jesus name.

3). I shall not be a disappointment to the body of Christ, in Jesus name.

4). As the Lord lives, I shall bring honor to the church, in Jesus name.

5). I shall not be a reproach to the house of God, in Jesus name.

6). Holy Spirit, guide me to walk in the footsteps of the Son of God, in Jesus name.

7). I receive the spirit of God to walk in patience, in Jesus name.

8). I terminate the authority of the spirit of anxiety over my life, in Jesus name.

9). Authority of powers contending with the joy of the lord in my life, expire today, in Jesus name.

10). I uproot the tree of arrogance in my foundation, in Jesus name.

11). O Lord, make me to overflow with the milk of kindness, in Jesus name.

12). God of compassion, visit me and favor me, in Jesus name.

13). I frustrate every power with mandate to mock my patience, in Jesus name.

14). By the cross of Jesus I crossover from bondage to freedom, in Jesus name.

CHAPTER

ELEVEN

Baptism with the Holy Spirit

The mystery of the person of the Holy Spirit can additionally be understood by looking at the unique role he played in establishing the church and the powerful impact he has played since then in equipping them with essential spiritual gifts for purposeful ministry and bounteous harvest.

> *"But ye shall receive power, after that the Holy Ghost is come upon you: and ye shall be witnesses unto me both in Jerusalem, and in Judea, and in Samaria, and unto the uttermost part of the earth" (Acts 1: 8)*

Jesus promised his disciples that they would receive power to witness for him after he returns to his Father. But he said they would not be endued with this power until they were baptized by the Holy Spirit. Christianity would indeed have become a relic of little historical relevance without this power.

And on that day of Pentecost after Christ's ascension to his Father, something extra-ordinary, unique and spectacular happened in Jerusalem. A dimension of power never experienced before was unleashed on Jesus' disciples. That was a land-mark event that symbolized the gradual handing over of the baton of the body of the Law and Justice to the custodians of the covenant of Grace and mercy.

It marked the fulfilling of the promise of the Father of pouring his Holy Spirit upon all flesh. Since that day, the Holy Spirit has played more helpful roles of dispensing spiritual gifts and enabling believers with supernatural power for accomplishing great works. And as a result, the work of Christ on earth has carried on successfully for more than two-thousand years.

By his divine power, he helps believers to do things right, and transforms ordinary people to accomplish extra-ordinary feats for Christ and God's kingdom. His un-imaginable power inspires courage and motivates boldness in converts to engage in ministry. And believers endowed with it receive ability to make disciples and the authority to carry on effective mission work.

Every descendant of Adam and Eve is considered to be born of sinful flesh. But after there is regeneration in any life as prompted by the convicting work of Holy Spirit, that individual commences a new life in Christ. This process is referred to in theological circles as the "New-birth" experience or "Being born-again".

This New-birth experience is also referred to as the conversion experience. This is because, it is literarily a conversion from the kingdom of darkness to the kingdom of light. It is a vital step that qualifies a sinner who has received Jesus as the son of God, to also receive a slot in eternal life with Christ, when he comes for his church.

"Verily, verily, I say unto you, He that heareth my word, and believeth on him that sent me, hath everlasting life, and shall not come into condemnation; but is passed from death unto life" (John 5: 24).

"Jesus saith to him, He that is washed needeth not save to wash his feet, but is clean every whit: and ye are clean, but not all" (John 13: 10).

So, apart Judas Iscariot whom Jesus indirectly described as unclean, many of Jesus' early disciples received this promise, prior to his glorification. Why? Because, they believed till the end, not only in the word that Jesus preached, but also in his Father who sent him.

But after the "New birth experience, comes another necessary work of the Holy Spirit which involves baptizing the New converts with power. In some cases, this Baptism of the Holy Spirit does occur immediately following the New birth experience. But this is not usually the case. So, it is more standard occurrence to find converts that are baptized in water but are not baptized yet in the Holy Spirit.

All men are born of sinful flesh having descended from Adam and Eve. But there is a regeneration by the Spirit of God that marks the commencement of a carnal person's walk with Christ. This experience is referred in theological circles as the "new-birth" or "being born-again".

When a person receives the new-birth experience, the Holy Spirit immediately takes up residence in that soul. This is commonly referred to as the "Indwelling of the Holy Spirit". Without his indwelling in a person of faith, Christians and the entire body of Christ will be unable to express, in any meaningful measure, the essence of Christ. In which case the concept of salvation becomes vain and of no doctrinal relevance.

But the term "Baptism with the Holy Ghost" however, is different. It represents a necessary second-influence by the Holy Spirit upon a converted soul. This second impact results in the bestowal of spiritual power on a person who is "born-again".

This must occur before any effective and fruitful ministry can take place.

For someone to be baptized with the Holy Ghost, as it is also described, that individual is presumed to have already been born-again. This requirement is a necessary condition for receiving this irrevocable gift and encounter. Even though a person's soul has to hunger for this encounter and desire this gift.

So, there is an indwelling of the Holy Spirit, as separate from the infilling with the Holy Spirit. While the indwelling of the Holy Spirit is the result of a person's salvation experience, the in-filling occurs simultaneously with the baptism with the Holy Ghost.

The "**indwelling**" of the Holy Spirit in a person, represents what happens immediately after the salvation experience occurs in that life. But the "**infilling**" by the Holy Ghost occurs after a person who is born-again receives the baptism of power. Both experiences come with divine benefits and privileges.

Quite often, Christians crave the in-filling of the Holy Ghost with their attention mainly focused on its benefits. They give little or no considerations to the sacrificial demands required to operate in its boldness and incredible power. A little lesson from the letter of Apostle Paul to the Philippians can be helpful here.

> *"That I may know him, and the power of his resurrection, and the fellowship of his sufferings, being made conformable unto his death; If by any means I might attain unto the resurrection of the dead. Not as though I had already attained, either were already perfect: but I follow after, if that I may apprehend that for which also I am apprehended of Christ Jesus. Brethren, I count not myself to have*

*apprehended: but this one thing I do, forgetting
those things which are behind, and reaching
forth unto those things which are before, I press
toward the mark for the prize of the high calling
of God in Christ Jesus (Philippians 3: 10-14).*

Believers who desire this awesome experience must first wean their souls of the condemnation of past guilts. They must be ready to focus on the new goal of chasing a life in Christ with undistracted fervor and sacrificial thrust. It is to those committed Christians whose lives conform to Christ's death this power of resurrection comes to easily without reservation. It is by the Holy Ghost baptism that this incredible power is conferred upon those believers who surrender their will to the absolute will of God.

*"The God of our fathers raised up Jesus, whom
ye slew and hanged on a tree. Him hath God
exalted with his right hand to be a Prince and
a Savior, for to give repentance to Israel, and
forgiveness of sins. And we are his witnesses of
these things, and so also is the Holy Ghost, whom
God hath given to them that obey" (Acts 5: 32).*

Christians who receive the Holy Ghost baptism are individuals who are broken in the spirit and who are very ready to release every area of their lives to God. No one, but God rules in such lives, as they are completely disconnected from the trappings of the flesh.

This baptism is such a beautiful spiritual experience that no Christian worth his faith should be left without it. But there must be the eagerness, hunger, readiness, and thirst for this refreshing river of life that flows from the deep wells of divine power.

This baptism by the Holy Spirit is inevitable for ministry.

It is vital for the manifestation of God's power by the body of Christ. Without this baptism, the church will be weak, powerless and unable to continue the work of Christ. And this can only be pleasant to the enemies of God.

The "Baptism with the Holy Ghost" is God's gift to the church which came in fulfilment of his promise through the prophets. God promised of a time when there will be an unrestricted outpouring of his Spirit upon all flesh and not just a privileged few.

Prior to the Day of Pentecost, the Holy Spirit operated only through a select few persons. These were mainly Prophets, Kings and Judges of the Hebrew extraction. But God gave some prophets the insight of a time when he will make the Holy Spirit available to believers all over the whole world, irrespective of their racial extraction, gender, age and status.

> *"And it shall come to pass afterward, that I will pour out my spirit upon all flesh; and your sons and your daughters shall prophesy, your old men shall dream dreams, your young men shall see visions: And also upon the servants and upon the handmaids in those days will I pour out my spirit" (Joel 2: 28-29).*

For anyone to be baptized by the Holy Spirit, that individual is presumed to have been born-again and has received water Baptism. It is an inheritance primarily reserved for those who unashamedly confess the Lord Jesus with their mouth and believe in their hearts that God raised him from the dead.

> *"That if thou shalt confess with thy mouth the Lord Jesus, and shalt believe in thine heart that God hath raised him from the dead, thou shalt be saved (Romans 10: 9).*

"In whom ye also trusted, after that ye heard the word of truth, the gospel of your salvation: in whom also after that ye believed, ye were sealed with that holy Spirit of promise, Which is the earnest of our inheritance until the redemption of the purchased possession, unto the praise of his glory" (Ephesians 1: 13-14).

While the indwelling of the Holy Spirit usually precedes the in-filling of the Holy Ghost as a standard rule, there are however a few occasions when infilling by the Holy Ghost occurred before the indwelling by the Holy Spirit. During these situations, the converts were filled by the Holy Spirit even before they received water baptism (John 20: 18-23; Acts 9: 15-18; acts 10: 34-46).

It is true that the Holy Ghost baptism and its benefits are the undeniable privileges of every child of faith by reason of their salvation experience, yet, it is something that must be sought after with humility, pursued with spiritual hunger, honest objective, total surrender to the will of God and the sincere desire to serve the church.

And Christians who are filled with the Holy Spirit, who long for the in-filling of the Holy Ghost or his baptism, must be determined to operate like spiritual pipes and not be like stagnant river. They must let the Holy Spirit readily flow through them, so that he can reach other people.

And those who have been sealed and filled with the Holy Spirit must continue to covet his baptism of power. It is the outpouring of his power that results in the speaking of other tongues. The believer who has received this experience must not allow to fade.

"And when the day of Pentecost was fully come, they were all with one accord in one place. And

suddenly there came a sound from heaven as of a rushing mighty wind, and it filled all the house where they were sitting. And there appeared unto them cloven tongues like as of fire, and it sat upon each of them. And they were all filled with the Holy Ghost, and began to speak with other tongues, as the Spirit gave them utterance" (Acts 2: 1-4).

The baptism of the Holy Spirit strengthens the believer's faith, resulting in boldness for ministry. This is in addition to the overflowing joy it provides the convert who is endowed with this power (Acts 4: 31; 13: 52). The Holy Spirit desires to possess every area of a believer's life and cannot wait to take up full and permanent residence in their body. That is why the Christian is described as his Temple. The Temple of God.

A Christian that is filled with the Holy Ghost, should always operate as he directs. He must not stifle him or resist the move of his power whenever there is a prompting. The Holy Spirit fills with supernatural power, so, he should be allowed to flow as he pleases.

Because this baptism is from God, it is expected that religious skeptics and secular critics will turn the children of faith who operate in his gifts to objects of ridicule. They will deride some, taunt others and mimic the rest. But no true Christian should allow himself to be humiliated by such mockery, persecution, or hatred, realizing what is at stake.

What the Christian who is baptized by the Holy Spirit possesses is an uncommon treasure from Christ. It is a precious treasure greater than silver, gold or diamond, which every believer should desire to have. That is why unbelievers scorn it. The benefits to the church however, are so invaluable to consider any consequences suffered for its sake. And soon, those that mocked you shall come to compliment you when they see the power of God move in your life.

The "Holy Spirit baptism", "Holy Ghost baptism", "Baptism in the Holy Ghost", "Baptism in the Holy Spirit", or "Baptism of fire", refer to the same and one experience. It is a baptism that unleashes power, boldness, and strength to accomplish great works for God and to overcome personal sin.

It releases the power of God into believers enabling them to continue the work of Christ. It is impossible to effectively express the character of God or bear Christ-like fruit without experiencing this baptism and receiving the delegated power that comes with it. So, the power that accompanies this baptism is not given for personal use or to be buried unused, but for appropriation to the glory of God.

This baptism equipped Jesus Christ during his earthly ministry to work the several miracles, signs, and wonders that evoked attention to his kingdom message. And it authenticated his claim not only as God sent, but as God's Son.

Baptism with the Holy Spirit is so titled because of its general association with the gifts of God. Through these gifts, God manifests himself to his children and to the church through the third person of the godhead. This supernatural baptism is usually an evidence of divine commendation showing that a Christian is ready enough to be trusted with spiritual power for the benefit of the church.

While the idea of the water baptism originally administered by John the Baptist, represented an outward cleansing for the forgiveness of sins, the Holy Spirit baptism typified an inward purging of the believer's soul with spiritual fire. This latter baptism endows believers with power, consecrating them for service in the kingdom of God.

This baptism is also not an automatic feeling experienced upon the new birth with a set time-frame for its occurrence, even though it is the convert's benefit of salvation. So, every Christian is encouraged to hunger, and thirst for it through prayer.

Like the phrase "Holy Trinity", the term "Baptism of the Holy Spirit" is not stated in the bible. In many places where it is encountered, it is used figuratively to describe an out-pouring of the Spirit of God during which he confers powerful benefits upon his children (Joel 2:28-29; Acts 1: 1-5; 2: 1-2).

The earliest illustration of this concept in the Bible refers to the incident directly related to the immersion, water-baptism of Jesus by John the Baptist. As Jesus stepped out of the River Jordan River, the bible says, he was concurrently baptized by the Holy Ghost.

Jesus was full of this power and accomplished great miracles, signs, and wonders because the Holy Spirit was with him. This is the power he promised to confer upon all those who believe in him or would come into faith in Christ earnestly desiring to serve in the kingdom of God.

And the scriptures testify that on the day of Pentecost, as the disciples gathered in the upper-room in Jerusalem, awaiting the promise of the Father, a sound described as "a mighty rushing wind" came down from heaven. That account in the "Book of the Acts of the Apostles" further confirm that as the unusual wind filled the entire room, there appeared immediately, cloven tongues looking like fire, which sat respectively on each disciple in that gathering.

"And when the day of Pentecost was fully come, they were all with one accord in one place. And suddenly there came a sound from heaven as

*of a rushing mighty wind, and it filled all the
house where they were sitting" (Acts 2: 1-2).*

This manifestation, no doubt, was in part fulfilment of some
of the numerous prophecies in the Old Testament concerning the
time of the out-pouring of the Holy Spirit. It also represented the
fulfillment of the promise of our Lord Jesus Christ to his disciples,
long before he was glorified. (Luke 3:16; Joel 2: 28-29).

In some scriptures, the baptism of the Holy Ghost is described
as a baptism of fire. This is a symbolic representation pointing to
a literal process of spiritual purging of an individual's soul with
fire. God uses spiritual-fire for a whole lot of purposes. Sometimes
he uses it as judgment for sin and in other cases, as a sign of his
presence to attract attention.

A Christian that is baptized in the Holy Ghost burns with
righteous zeal and always radiates with the power of God.
Christians whose hearts are kindled with Holy-fire are generally
comfortable with affecting other souls with their flame. They are
the believers feared by the Devil because of the flames they carry
for Christ.

A Christian hungry to do the will of God will ultimately
be filled with the power of the Holy Spirit. But it is sad that
such Christians are no-longer easy to find. It is a tragedy of
ironic dimensions to observe the extent to which many "Christian
alcoholics" and drug addicts go to get a drink of alcohol or sniff
a line of cocaine, just to get momentarily high.

The result is that these victims, in their deranged minds,
get involved in foolish and reckless acts that dishonor God and
bring reproach to the church. In a confused state of mind, an
alcoholic is useless to himself and most useless to the church
and his society. For this reason, the Bible admonishes Christians
against alcoholism

"See then that ye walk circumspectly, not as fools, but as wise, Redeeming the time, because the days are evil. Wherefore be ye not unwise, but understanding what the will of the Lord is. And be not drunk with wine, wherein is excess; but be filled with the Spirit; (Ephesians 5:15-18).

If faithful believers will hunger and thirst for the Holy Spirit, taking same steps in search for him as addicts do to get high on alcohol and drugs, the church will be so drunk in the Holy Ghost and in constant "spiritual high". A congregation of God's children in this spiritual mode will powerfully overcome whatever the enemy throws at the church and readily take on and destroy any evil works of darkness.

The baptism with the Holy Spirit is still available. It is God's fulfilled promise to the church and Christ encourages his disciples to experience it. It is thus the responsibility of every Christian to take advantage of this offer by getting baptized in the Holy Spirit.

The Holy Spirit and Power.

There are so-many privileges that benefit a Christian in good relationship with the Holy Spirit. One of them is friendship with the divine Trinity. The Bible describes Jesus as "the good shepherd". A good shepherd takes good care of his sheep. He feeds them with the best food and gives them drink from cleanest, clearest and most calm waters. A Christian in good relationship with the Holy Spirit will regularly enjoy these good things that pertain to life and godliness.

In seeking for the good life, the believer must focus on meaningful things that matter to God and his kingdom. This is because a Christian that has all things but lacks Jesus, lacks everything. A life without Jesus cannot walk in righteousness. And in that case, such a soul will not find God's peace or experience the joy of the Holy Ghost.

> *"For the kingdom of God is not meat and drink; but righteousness, and peace, and joy in the Holy Ghost" (Romans 14: 17).*

A soul without Christ and the Holy Spirit is in great danger of constantly experiencing crises. So, while it is alright to aspire for the abundant life which Christ provided, the most gainful possession in life is to have Christ and be possessed by the Holy Spirit.

So, every Christian needs the Holy Spirit. He motivates those who he possesses to keep regular schedule with God and to walk in divine appointment with Christ. And he helps them to boldly enter into the throne of grace where they obtain mercy and grace to help in time of need (Hebrews 4:16).

No one is beyond the reach of God. But the Holy Spirit is that necessary link through Christ the Son, to God the Father. He is the inevitable socket through which a believer can connect to the divine power of the Holy Trinity. Any child of faith that is not in touch with the Holy Spirit cannot effectively connect to the will of God. He is the link to the altars of forgiveness, graces, mercies and other favors.

Nothing in this natural world can impact an individual more than the influence the Holy Spirit. That is why it is such an incredible honor to be indwelled by him and baptized with his power. This all starts with the process of the salvation experience which he initiates. Thereafter, comes the baptism with the with the Spirit of God. All these experiences are very phenomenal.

It is through interaction with the Holy Spirit that a Christian can enjoy unhindered access to the mind of God, enjoy liberty in Christ, receive power to deal with sin and obtain the boldness and authority to destroy the wicked works of darkness. He is the divine carrier of supernatural anointing and the easiest means for receiving ultimate power to save, serve, heal, deliver, prosper, revive, and restore people.

Once a Christian encounter's the Holy Spirit and is baptized, everything changes in that life. Nothing remains the same again. The Holy Spirit is a good spirit and the secret to divine power. Every Christian needs to encounter him in order to accomplish supernatural feats.

A Christian who receives his power is able to subdue all problems. Sicknesses surrender before him, bondages and yokes break at his command and demons quickly bow, as he mentions the name of Jesus. They crush serpents and scorpions commonly and charms are easily rendered impotent at their command.

King David understood the benefits of a Holy Spirit-indwelt life and his gracious influences. No wonder he magnified him as the custodian of divine power, extoled him as source of the joy of salvation and praised him as the one who gives power against temptation and sin.

So, after he followed the inclination of his carnal soul and sinned, in the matter of Bathsheba, he knew he had grieved the Holy Spirit. And knowing the consequences of such act, he prayed for forgiveness, asking that God spare him the gift, power and presence of his Holy Spirit.

"Against thee, thee only, have I sinned, and done this evil in thy sight: that thou mightest be justified when thou speakest, and be clear when thou judgest.Behold, I was shapen in

iniquity; and in sin did my mother conceive me" (Psalms 51: 4-5).

David sinned with Bathsheba and in the process Uriah, Bathsheba's husband was killed. Both acts were sins against God. No one was there when King David committed the unlawful act of extra-marital sex with Bathsheba. But the Holy Spirit who has the power to know and see all-things convicted him of the sin. And because he knew it would cost him, he cried out to God. And when he did, God restored fellowship with him.

> *"Make me to hear joy and gladness; that the bones which thou hast broken may rejoice. Hide thy face from my sins, and blot out all mine iniquities. Create in me a clean heart, O God; and renew a right spirit within me. Cast me not away from thy presence; and take not thy holy spirit from me. Restore unto me the joy of thy salvation; and uphold me with thy free spirit" (Psalm 51: 8- 12).*

The Holy Spirit requires nothing before he can fill a thirsty soul. He does not demand for talent, beauty, or strength, and does not carry out background checks or pre-qualify persons by their fame, fortune or greatness before using them. Instead, he empowers those who are thirsty for him with the necessary power for ministry, fellowship and friendship.

The presence of the Holy Spirit in a Christian's life takes that individual from just being a nominal believer to becoming a phenomenal child of God. When he possesses an ordinary but willing, person of faith, he transforms him into an extra-ordinary child of God with power to accomplish extra-ordinary feats.

Nothing remarkable can happen in a believer's life or ministry without the intervention of the Holy Spirit. For this reason, those who desire to be used by God must yearn to be baptized by his Spirit. His is still available to baptize willing and righteous converts with power and divine gifts to accomplish God's agenda for the church.

Through the power of the Holy Spirit, the believer is literarily able to move mountains and cause impossibilities to become possible. He is the spiritual dynamite that turns believers into uncommon way-makers and trail-blazers. But no person can truly operate in this supernatural power without first acknowledging the work of Christ or appreciating the selfless sacrifice that set up the earthly platform upon which the humble Holy Spirit now reigns supreme.

The message of the entire bible is about Jesus the Son of God, to whom the Holy Spirit serves as witness. As a result, the power that Christians receive from the Holy Spirit is to enable them become witnesses also for Christ and by so doing, be revealed to the hearts of perishing souls and deliver them.

The Holy Spirit remains the undisputed secret to success in any Christian's life. He is God's principal agent for making converts and the divine ambassador that prepares witnesses and disciples for Christ. By his acts, he establishes believers as undeniable beacons of light so they can shine brightly even in the darkest of places of the earth.

This is when something profound and supernatural begin to happen through those lives as they help to bring God's plan for mankind into focus. One such experience can last a life-time. It was responsible for the encounter that turned the persecuting Saul of Tarsus into a zealous apostle Paul, the disciple of Christ.

That is why people who honestly desire the power of God must first know and acknowledge the persons of the divine Trinity. Apostle Paul was learned in the law of Moses. His knowledge of the divine Deity was limited to the God of the Sinai, which all Jews worshipped at his time. And even though this knowledge revealed the future Jesus, it did not teach much about the Holy Spirit.

But when the time came and he encountered the power of the Holy Spirit, the life of this astute lawyer that once persecuted Christ's followers, and who trained under Gamaliel the renowned Jewish custodian of the law, changed completely. Profound and supernatural things began to happen in his life and ministry.

This is why every committed Christian must be hungry for an encounter with the Holy Spirit. The result of one such experience will last a life-time. No one can encounter the Holy Spirit and remain the same. He changes lives and brings out the best in anyone he touches. His power validates a ministry, and authenticates God's calling on a life. He baptizes those he calls with the power to function, consecrates them for service and transforms them into weapons of warfare.

Sadly, the devil is currently counterfeiting his power and using it to seduce the world. In some modern Pentecostal gatherings for instance, congregants are taught to mimic manifestations framed after the gifts of the Holy Spirit. And in these places, magical tricks are staged as miracles in the satanic effort to entice souls and keep humanity in bondage.

The devil has perfected his art of deception through false prophets, healers, and deliverance agents. And over time, he has employed them in accomplishing the evil purpose of weakening the church. And unfortunately, many "so-called Christians" are falling for these seductions in the hot pursuit for quick miracles and wonders.

In this sadly confused church era, it is not surprising to see the Devil or his agents operating in places where children of God gather, like he did in the time of the patriarch Job. He still employs the same old tactics he used and is no less a conspicuous participant in Church congregation activities today, as he was in the past.

> *"Now there was a day when the sons of God came to present themselves before the Lord, and Satan came also among them. And the Lord said unto Satan, Whence comest thou? Then Satan answered the Lord, and said, From going to and fro in the earth, and from walking up and down in it" (Job 1: 6-7).*

In this modern generation, this man of perdition now receives higher honor in many gatherings called "churches". In those places, he operates unchallenged as leader, glaringly promoting his worldly doctrines to levels that were unthinkable in the days of the apostles. In fact, he boldly preaches via several pulpits from where he is hailed for his lying signs, miracles and wonders.

The Devil operates by unrighteous power. Unfortunately, many people of faith have sold their hearts to him. Others, in admiration of his fraudulent methods, have fallen for his tricks, learned his techniques, and now employ them as useful tools in their covens, shrines and worship-altars. This explains why he has been very successful of late, flagrantly flaunting his demonic power, publicly perverting righteous moral laws, and caging the souls of mankind, including of course, many people who once confessed their faith in Christ.

However, through the operation of the Holy Spirit, the righteous in Christ can rise again with supernatural power to subdue the enemy and his works of darkness. Without this power, all mankind will continue to live under satanic manipulation, oppression and control.

The Church needs to operate afresh in this power that has

potential to deliver souls from the cages of wickedness. Under the influence of this power, illiterate, fishermen built great ministries and became bold, respected spiritual mega-phones for Christ and fearless spokes-persons for God. They achieved all these by the power of the Holy Spirit and succeeded in turning the world upside-down for Jesus. This is still possible today as the same Holy Spirit still rules and reigns like he did in the past.

PRAYER POINTS.

1). O Lord, do not cast me away from your presence, in Jesus name.

2). My Father, do not take away your Holy Spirit from me, in Jesus name.

3). O God, restore the joy of your salvation unto me, in Jesus name.

4). O Lord, renew your right spirit within my soul, in Jesus name.

5). O God lift me up from the dust and set my feet on the solid rock, in Jesus name.

6). Oasis in the desert, give drink to my thirsty soul, in Jesus name.

7). My father, even in the slippery slope, I trust you will hold me up, in Jesus name.

8). Holy ghost fire, consume the evil powers contending with my destiny, in Jesus name.

9). Holy Spirit, give me a mind for deep understanding, in Jesus name.

10). Holy Spirit, open my eyes to perceive the benefits of heaven from the earth, in Jesus name.

11). Holy Spirit, strengthen me with might in my inner man, in Jesus name.

12). O Lord, grant me the riches of your glory, in Jesus name.

13). Holy Spirit, help me to know the love of Christ, in Jesus name.

14). Holy Spirit, help me to be part of this end-time harvest, in Jesus name.

TWELVE

The Christian, the Church and the Holy Spirit

The Christian is a unique kind of person. He is an individual delivered from the bondage of the devil where he was once bound because of his personal sins or his blood-line abominations. Before conversion, all Christians were sinners. But by the righteous works of Jesus on the cross, all Christians were redeemed.

So, the Christian was once a condemned soul whom God saved from the yoke of wickedness and the unkind-chains of the kingdom of darkness. He was someone destined to die but was purchased from the jaws of death with the precious blood of Jesus, rescued at the cross and given a second chance at life.

Following this rescue from Satan, and consequent induction into the family of Christ, a Christian convert is not expected to live in the mess of his old nature. Instead, he is supposed, by the requirement of his new-nature, to comport himself under the righteous standards of purity and holiness in line with the prevailing tenets of the family of Christ.

Although he still lives in the natural world, he is no longer expected to conform to the carnal demands of its broken system. Rather, he is supposed to embrace a new pattern of life defined by the constant renewing of his mind in God's word and in the deliberately obedience to God's commandments.

The responsibility for a pure, holy and sacrificial life is an honorable choice which every committed Christian with the fear of God should make. These choices are acts of the will and constitute evidences of a life that is determined to model Christ to the world.

None of these can be accomplished without the indwelling help of the Holy Spirit. It is the Holy Spirit's charge to teach people of faith the art of knowing and doing God's will in ways that are pleasant to him. He leads believers in all truth and guides them in the way of light.

The Holy Spirit is the fulfillment of God's promise for his people, which he spoke through the prophets in ancient times. And throughout Bible-history, there is a progressive revelation of his person, until that special Pentecost when he fully manifested upon the church.

Since that special Feast of harvests known also as Feast of Pentecost, He has remained the supernatural presence of God who is resident in all believers. From there, he establishes God's desire through them in the body of Christ, faithfully guiding their fragile steps as they walk in the new life of adopted children of God.

Through his numerous virtues, he enables believers to walk daily in love, helping them also to bear Christ-like fruit. His presence in believers authenticates their genuine claim to the membership of the Body of Christ, a claim that qualifies them to enjoy the same privileges with Christ, as (adopted) children of God.

The Holy Spirit is the fulfilled promise of God that came to the church on the day of Pentecost. In Judaism, the "Feast of Pentecost" is an ancient religious festival known also as the "Festival of Weeks".

This festival is celebrated seven weeks and one day after the Sabbath following the feast of Passover. It is a Jewish ceremony marking the giving the Torah to Moses at Mount Sinai and usually falls on the day of the summer, wheat-harvest.

The full manifestation of the Holy Spirit upon the disciples of Jesus coincided with one such Pentecost. It was on one such Jewish festival that this phenomenal event in Bible-history occurred. And perfectly in line with the promise of God, which he spoke many years before, through Old Testament prophets, this event occurred before many witnesses.

> *"And it shall come to pass afterward, that I will pour out my spirit upon all flesh; and your sons and your daughters shall prophesy, your old men shall dream dreams, your young men shall see visions: And also upon the servants and upon the handmaids in those days will I pour out my spirit" (Joel 2: 28-29).*

On this particular "Feast of Pentecost", as Christ's disciples now numbering about one hundred and twenty, gathered in prayer at the upper room in Jerusalem, there came a sudden sound from heaven. This unprecedented occurrence in the form of a mighty rushing wind, came and filled all the upper-room where the disciples assembled, as they waited in prayers for the gift of the Father.

> *"And when the day of Pentecost was fully come, they were all with one accord in one place. And suddenly there came a sound from heaven as of a rushing mighty wind, and it filled all*

the house where they were sitting. And there appeared unto them cloven tongues like as of fire, and it sat upon each of them. And they were all filled with the Holy Ghost, and began to speak with other tongues, as the Spirit gave them utterance" (Acts 2: 1-4).

This wind, which appeared as cloven tongues of fire settled upon each of the disciples. And every one of them present on that occasion experienced this novel touch of God and spoke in irrefutable foreign tongues, which was a clear evidence of the baptism with Holy Spirit.

From that moment, that incredible experience ignited an insatiable hunger in many Jews and Gentiles for what Christ taught. It also kindled a blazing spiritual fire in Jerusalem which the religious leaders tried without fail to extinguish. Instead, from the ashes of this fire grew an unprecedented number of home churches across the entire Roman Empire. And as more persecution arose against Christ's disciples, many of them fled into the regions of Judea, Samaria, and other parts of the earth, primarily in search of refuge but in fulfilment of Christ's word (Matthew 28: 18-20).

Yet the vicious threats from older and more established religious groups did not stop as numerous cult leaders and self-appointed religious activists of that era jumped into the fray against these disciples. These deadly affronts and violent attacks became the evil hallmarks of that period as many of Christ's disciples and converts became ostracized by family, friends and society while more suffered martyrdoms as a result of their new-found faith.

The church is rightly described as living in the age of the Holy Spirit. Which is to say that the church was born through physical revelation of his power. And from the moment the church was born, she has continued, till this day, to benefit from the wholesome manifestation of power of the Holy Spirit.

The teachings of Christ as continued by the disciples were very simple and easily attracted followers. But the teachers of the law presented it to the people as contradictory the doctrines of the law which the scribes and Pharisees held as sacrosanct. So, this created more problems to the disciple. So, while the manifestations by the Holy Spirit came with power, grace and gifts, it left indelible marks on the lives of those early disciples most of whom never survived.

In the Old Testament, the law was written on tablets of stone. But in this new dispensation, God chose to reveal himself directly to his people by his Spirit that now lives inside of them. Thus, the law which in the Old covenant was engraved on tablets of stones, is now in this dispensation, inscribed on human hearts of God's children, by his Holy Spirit.

Sadly, only a few Christians appreciate the value of the great spiritual power that resides inside of them. Many Christians do not even realize what they miss because they have no knowledge of his nature and attributes, or how to relate with him in order to appropriate his gifts and power.

As a result of this ignorance, Christians continue to struggle in darkness, searching for power in places where it does not exist. By so doing the church loses unreasonably from the numerous benefits of the Holy Spirit, to the delight of the Devil who must be surprised at how easy it has become to defraud believers of their heritage for which Christ died.

By the righteousness of Christ and the mercies of God, all Christians qualify to operate in the power and gifts of the Holy Spirit. This was the situation in the early church era. He was the power that authenticated the faith of those early disciples, transformed the new-converts, and inculcated in them the godly attitude that helped them walk in love, joy, peace and a sound mind.

This is why the Holy Spirit is relevant in every believer's life. He is the link the Christian requires to bond with God. When there is no such connection, the believer is powerless, crippled and helpless, as nothing in the life of a person can succeed only by human effort.

The gifts of the Holy Spirit are meant for the body of Christ. The Church is cheated by the Devil when supernatural gifts lie dormant or the power of the Holy Spirit is under-utilized in the church.

This explains why Christians who do not operate in the gifts and power of the Holy Spirit need to covet them. And for those who already possess these gifts, they must ensure they put them to practical use to the glory of God and not just flaunt them.

The troubling nature of our depraved society, as well as huge spiritual issues Christians regularly encounter in life are enough reasons for a closer relationship with the Father, the Son, and the Holy Spirit. Without this close relationship with the Holy Trinity, the body of Christ will be vulnerable to the vicious attacks by the workers of darkness.

The church was born out of God's love for perishing souls and his kindness to suffering humanity. This includes you, me, all Christians and those that have yet to give their lives to him. But it is tragic that only few Christians fully appreciate the sacrifice that established her structure. If believers really knew this, more people will adopt apostle Paul's approach after he came to Christ.

The Spirit of God was so alive in him that a man who spent most of his time persecuting Christians had to sacrifice the rest of his life to unashamedly embrace the gospel which he once disdained. From the moment he accepted Christ, the power of the

Holy Spirit worked so much in him that he risked all for God's kingdom. To him, life was worth nothing if it did not include being crucified with Christ.

> *"I am crucified with Christ: nevertheless I live; yet not I, but Christ liveth in me: and the life which I now live in the flesh I live by the faith of the Son of God, who loved me, and gave himself for me" (Galatians 2: 20)*

> *"That I may know him, and the power of his resurrection, and the fellowship of his sufferings, being made conformable unto his death" Philippians 3; 10).*

The apostle Paul realized God's love for an imperfect being like himself. And from the moment of his conversion and Holy Spirit baptism, he became fully committed to the ways of Christ. He made selfless sacrifice to God's kingdom despite the many afflictions he experienced and the risks to his life.

He did not only embrace Christ's suffering-steps that provided him with eternal salvation but was also determined to experience that power (of the Holy Spirit) that raised Christ from the dead. This is the path of godliness that sustains spiritual power in the church. Only the Holy Spirit can inspire and enable a person with the full knowledge of its bitter implication, to live such a life of sacrifice.

Christians who enjoy deep relationship and regular fellowship with the Holy Trinity already possess the blessed satisfaction of heaven in their lives. For such believers, the demonstration of divine power is a common occurrence in their daily walk with Christ.

Intimacy with God comes into play when there is sweet

fellowship with the Holy Spirit. This friendship is not automatic but is formed by deliberate hunger for spiritual gifts and the selfless desire to have God's power made manifest through Christians to the advantage of the body of Christ and to the glory of God.

It is by regular fellowship with God in his word, in prayer, and by meditating in that word that any believer will attract the abundant riches of divine glory. Yet, all these only flow through the vessel of the Holy Spirit. So, it is under his control that the Christian and the Church are abundantly blessed.

The Church needs to have more than just an intellectual knowledge of God's word, a casual feeling of his love to deal with the issues of this complex age. Relationship with him needs to be in excess of the usual pedestrian affection before he can move in this age like he did in the early church. The believer's suffering is not expected to equal that of Christ. But there has to be sacrifice that is enough to attract the attention of God.

Any level of fellowship with Christ that desires the presence and power of the Holy Spirit, must involve fear of God, sacrificial love for others, total self-surrender, and zeal to win souls. Without these virtues which the Holy Spirit inspires, the Holy Spirit will not be involved in the worship.

The baptism of the Holy Spirit is one major gift that any serious Christian should covet. It is key to supreme sacrifice and supernatural power. It is a mystery once hidden by God, but now revealed in this church for purposeful service in God's vine-yard.

The Holy Spirit blesses believers with spiritual gifts through this baptism, so they can in return be channels of blessings to the Church. God expects the gifts he endows on his children to be put into regular use and not lay fallow. Because at any time and place, some Christian or church will have need of them.

When the early church was blessed with this gift, she was filled with joy and burnt with zeal. With this, the early disciples effectively shared their experience as they took the gospel beyond the borders of Jerusalem, Judea, and Samaria. And as they did, signs, miracles and wonders followed.

The Holy Spirit endows Christians with supernatural authority, boldness, courage, and confidence to witness in extraordinary ways that yield irrefutable results. The gifts enable believers to show what God can do through Holy Spirit-baptized Christians.

It must be stressed that supernatural gifts are not pre-requisite for making heaven. And while they are irrevocable, the believer who abuses his gift, backslides or renounces his faith, having once operated in the incredible power, will not inherit God's kingdom.

The modern Church needs the presence and power of the Holy Spirit as in the days of the early church. The continued presence of his power will enable the church to receive genuine insight into the mind of God and produce godly fruit. And the modern church needs to continually operate in this power as evidence that Jesus is still alive.

In the absence of the Holy Spirit, there will be no real link between militant saints on earth and Christ. The consequence of this will be a gathering of carnal "brides" un-prepared for the groom, at his appearance for the "marriage supper of the Lamb".

And without the role of the Holy Spirit, Christians will remain strangers to the common wealth of God's kingdom and vulnerable preys to the Devil. There will be no helper, no comforter, no counsellor or intercessor, and the church will be as weak as a helpless monument that can be uprooted by a rebellious child.

But thank God for the Holy Spirit. Because, the same power that sealed the disciples in the early church, is still working the present-day gathering of God's children. And the power that led to enormous growth during the early church-movement, is still doing the same today. In the past, he inspired illiterate disciples with a gospel that turned the world up-side down. He is still empowering souls for Christ in this electronic age.

> *"And he saw that there was no man, and wondered that there was no intercessor: therefore his arm brought salvation unto him; and his righteousness, it sustained him" (Isaiah 59: 16).*

It is the Holy Spirit that makes the difference between a Christian's sinful past, and his present redeemed life. He is the agent of God through whom Christ saves the transgressors from the deadness of their sins, giving them boldness and access to the throne of God.

Through the work of the Holy Spirit, all people of faith are reconciled with the Father through the Cross. They get adopted as sons and become joint heirs with Christ. This way, they can become consecrated as priests of an eternal covenant, are inducted citizens of heaven and receive access to the joyful presence of the God of all flesh.

Christ's message to the true church whereby signs, miracles and wonders happen today, confirm the active presence of the Holy Spirit and the manifestations of his power. Where he shows up, genuine healings, authentic deliverance, verifiable miracles of general prosperity and restorations occur. The church grows in spiritual knowledge and numerical strength, and God is glorified.

Christians fully possessed by the Holy Spirit enjoy spending time in the presence God. They value every session of prayer, bible study, quiet-time, worship, and appreciate true fasting. That is why all believers in Christ must covet and experience this third person of the divine Trinity.

Knowing the Holy Spirit is needful in acquiring the secret to Jesus' miracles, signs and wonders. This is because, everything that Christ accomplished were with the influence and power of the Holy Spirit. He is the supernatural instrument of God that makes impossibilities to become possible in the lives of those that believe.

He was behind Jesus' manifestation through the virgin conception and the power that sustained him throughout his earthly life and ministry. He strengthened him during his hours of persecution and judgment, comforted him while he agonized on the cross, and played a major role in his resurrection from the dead.

The Holy Spirit is God's gift to the Church to lead her into place of joy, peace, faith, patience, and love. He is the inevitable power for prayer, gives strength during temptation and nourishes the Christian during times of fasting. He is the believer's light in darkness and lends help in hopeless situations.

A Christian indwelt by the Holy Spirit becomes the complete image and likeness of God. Such a person becomes a reservoir of divine characters and virtues of God, desiring righteousness with passion and hating sin with perfect hatred. That is why Christian must covet his indwelling presence.

Where the Holy Spirit is accepted with awe and reverence, he inspires true worship, humbly guiding, cautiously guarding and patiently leading that believer into richer supernatural encounters that only committed and totally surrendered Christians can experience.

Christians filled with the Holy Spirit and who walk before the Lord with all their hearts, more often experience a greatly increased aura of the divine presence, glory, power, and activity of God. Their lives radiate Christ's love, gentleness, kindness, and mercy, and they literally swim in the peaceful-river of joy which no circumstances can influence.

They are lovely, compassionate, and humble people, patient

with all persons, faithful in their dealings with believers and unbelievers alike and bask in exceeding peace that is beyond human understanding. And most importantly, their lives represent a true reflection of Christ, The Messiah.

PRAYER POINTS.

1). Glory of the living Christ, fill the church, in Jesus name.

2). O God that knows all and sees all things, speak solution into my situation, in Jesus name.

3). Rock of Ages, collide with the powers causing me grief, in Jesus name.

4). Holy Spirit, expose, disgrace and destroy the powers causing havoc in my life, in Jesus name.

5). Voice of the blood of Jesus, silence the voice speaking problems into my life, in Jesus name.

6). Hand of God, lift me out of the miry pit, in Jesus name.

7). Shield of faith, protect me from the ancestral curse operating against my life, in Jesus name.

8). Holy Ghost fire destroy the plan to turn my destiny into rags, in Jesus name.

9). Lion of Judah, consume the evil lions threatening devour my life, in Jesus name.

10). Sun of righteousness, appear with healing for my sake, in Jesus name.

11). Holy Spirit, help me to fix my eyes on heavenly matters, in Jesus name.

12). God of creation, repair whatever sin has destroyed in my life, in Jesus name.

13). God of signs and wonders perform your wonders in my life, in Jesus name.

14). Father, Son and Holy Spirit, lead me where I should go, in Jesus name.

Printed in the United States
By Bookmasters